T0273689

CLUEDLE

THE CASE OF THE
DUMPLETON DIAMOND

CLUEDLE

THE CASE OF THE
DUMPLETON
DIAMOND

HARTIGAN BROWNE

WORKMAN PUBLISHING • NEW YORK

Copyright © 2024 by Hartigan Browne

Workman Kids
Workman Publishing
Hachette Book Group, Inc.
1290 Avenue of the Americas
New York, NY 10104
workman.com

Workman Kids is an imprint of Workman Publishing, a division of Hachette Book Group, Inc.
The Workman name and logo are registered trademarks of Hachette Book Group, Inc.

Design by Daniella Graner and Jennifer Keenan
Photo credits: Shutterstock

Workman books may be purchased in bulk for business, educational, or promotional use.
For information, please contact your local bookseller or the Hachette Book Group
Special Markets Department at special.markets@hbgusa.com.

ISBN 978-1-5235-3163-9

Ebook ISBNs 978-1-5235-3164-6, 978-1-5235-3165-3, 978-1-5235-3166-0

First Edition July 2024 VER

Originally published in the UK by Macmillan Children's Books,
an imprint of Pan Macmillan, in 2024.

Printed in Illinois, USA, on responsibly sourced paper.

10 9 8 7 6 5 4 3 2

LOOK OUT FOR

Hartigan's Hint

Evidence Log

[HARTIGAN BROWNE'S] CASE FILE

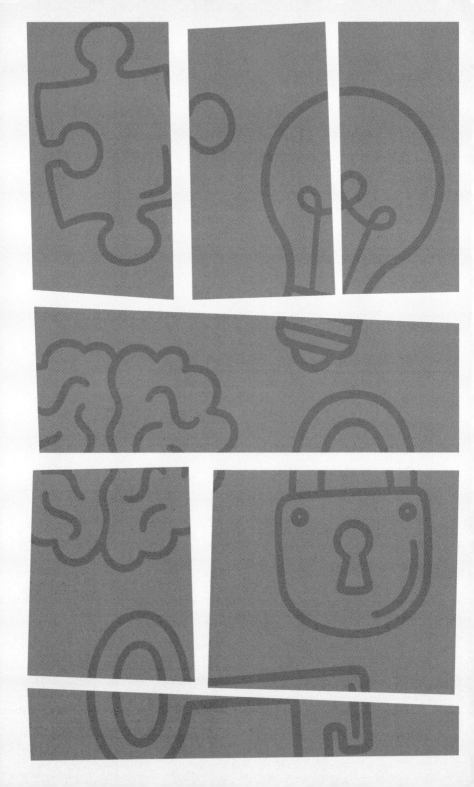

AGENT SELECTION

My name is Hartigan Browne, and I am looking for a recruit to join my detective agency. My instincts, which are rarely wrong, are telling me that you are the intelligent sort, which is fortunate, because only the sharpest and most brilliant minds need apply.

But, Hartigan, are you not the world's greatest private investigator? I hear you say. *Why do you need an assistant?* An excellent question, and the answer is that there are simply too many mysteries for one person to tackle. Business is booming and that's why I need someone like you to get to the bottom of all the crimes that are reported to me.

Now, I can't let you head off into the world of sleuthing without checking that you are indeed in possession of a sharp and brilliant mind. Therefore, you will need to complete four tasks to prove you have what it takes.

I have every confidence that you will be successful.

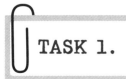

TASK 1.

For this task you need to reveal a secret message. Every shape in the code key stands for one letter of the alphabet. Fill in the answer by writing the matching letter above each shape.

Answer on page 172

CODE KEY

A	B	C	D	E	F
□	◇	△	◭	⬠	⬠

G	H	I	J	K	L
◹	⧓	◁	▽	◸	▷

M	N	O	P	Q	R
◿	◁	▱	▽	◹	⬡

S	T	U	V	W	X
▱	⊓	⋈	⋔	◺	◁

Y	Z
△	Σ

Well, that's a relief, no dunderheads here!

TASK 2.

You need to determine whether **Gear A** must be turned clockwise or counterclockwise in order for the pointer on the final gear to push the button on the printer. To find the answer, use a pencil to draw the direction the gears will turn. Remember that the direction one cog moves affects the one after it! Circle the correct direction.

Circle the direction that Gear A must turn:

CLOCKWISE   COUNTERCLOCKWISE

 HARTIGAN'S HINT:

Answer on page 173

Now print out* and fill in your name on your *Agent in Training* identity card, so you are able to investigate active cases.

Well done! How's that for some excellent *cog*nition? I'm sending you out into the field! You will need to work out the location of your very first case.

Print your card at hachettebookgroup.com/cluedle

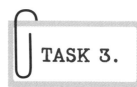

TASK 3.

The village you are being deployed to appears on the map below.

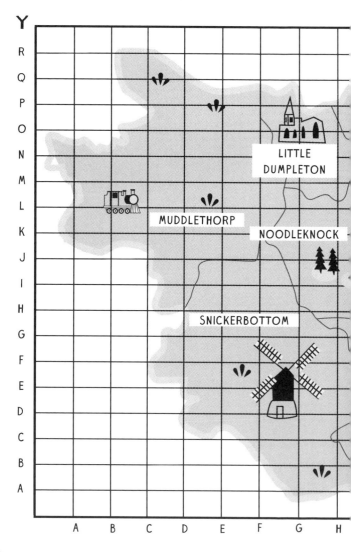

 HARTIGAN'S HINT: There is a clue in the task instruction as to which coordinates you require.

Use the coordinates to determine where you have to GO using the **x-** (horizontal) and **y-** (vertical) **axes** on the map. If you get stuck, remember that to find a location using coordinates, the **x-axis** comes first, then **y**. Once you have discovered your destination, circle it.

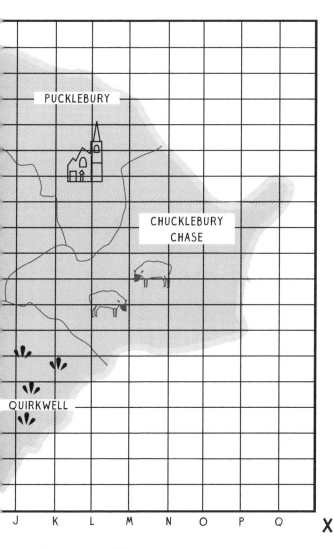

Answer on page 174

Haha! By Jove, you've cracked it! There was a rather large clue on the cover of this book, so I would have been surprised if you hadn't. But yes, you are off to Little Dumpleton, a charming village in Rompingshire. This town has experienced a troubling spate of wrongdoings ranging from stolen puppies and blackmail to . . . dun . . . dun . . . dun . . . attempted murder! This once sleepy village has become a hotbed of crime, and your services are required to discover the perpetrators of these heinous acts.

You're going to need my case notes to get up to speed. A good detective is always well prepared and well-informed (and, in my case, well-groomed—that is a preference and not a necessity, but do feel free to run a comb through your hair before you embark).

TASK 4.

To read the case notes, you will need to unlock my briefcase, which has been locked with a very special key card. Inserting the correct pattern into the slot at the bottom will release the locking mechanism. You must determine whether you need to insert pattern A or pattern B into the slot. The section on the front of the briefcase must match up with a section of either A or B. If you get it wrong, this book will explode.*

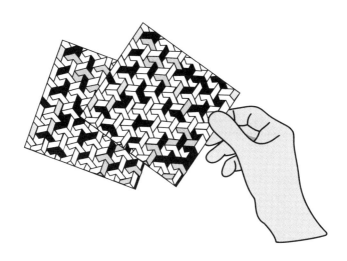

* This is a lie. I'm not in the habit of blowing up books. As a detective, you'll have to keep an eye out for untruths.

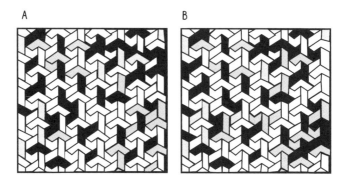

A   B

The answer is pattern: _____

 HARTIGAN'S HINT: The pattern on the
suitcase may be rotated 180 degrees.

Answer on page 175

Notes and deductions:

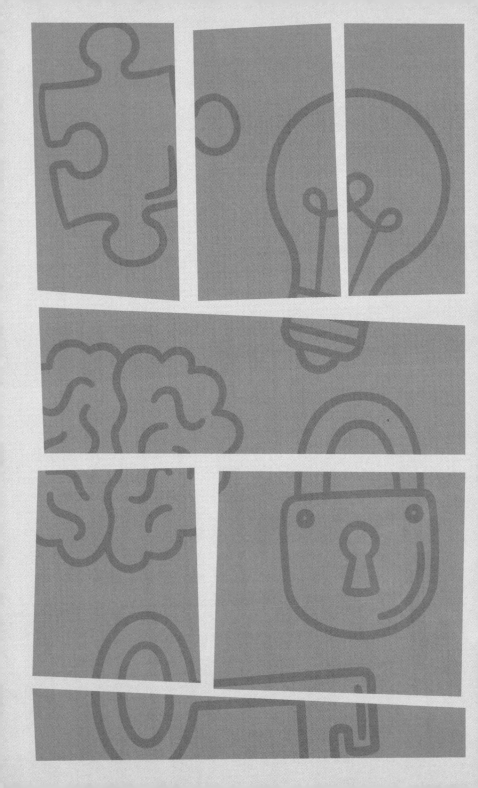

CASE 1:
PUP, PUP, AND AWAY!

C ongratulations, you opened the case notes! Read them with care:

It was a Tuesday afternoon when Ivanna Craft, owner of the Little Dumpleton art gallery, The Drawing Dump, knocked on my door. She was clearly distraught: red, blotchy eyes from crying, snotty nose—the works.

I put down my oboe (all proper detectives play a musical instrument, so pay attention in your recorder or ukulele lessons) and gestured for her to take a seat at my desk.

"Dave has been taken!" she told me.

"Who is Dave?" I asked, my interest piqued.

"My dog! Someone has pup-napped him."

Now, one must always consider the most obvious possibilities, so I said, "Are you sure you didn't lose him? Or perhaps he ran away?"

Ivanna didn't seem to think this was the case. "Dave would never leave me, and I would never lose him! He's my first pet and I love him!" she responded, quite hotly, and I felt she was telling the truth.

"What makes you think that he was taken?" I asked.

She pulled out a strap of some kind from her pocket and held it up. "He was tied up and someone cut his leash."

I examined the leash. It did indeed appear to have been cut. This is what the end of it looked like:

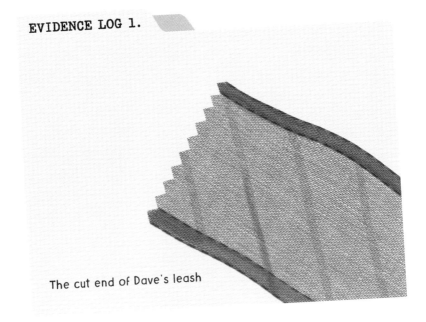

EVIDENCE LOG 1.

The cut end of Dave's leash

"And then . . . there's this!" she said. She took a crumpled piece of paper from her bag and passed it to me.

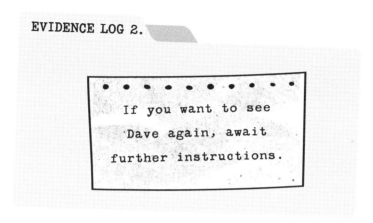

EVIDENCE LOG 2.

> If you want to see
> Dave again, await
> further instructions.

A ransom note! In our line of work, ransom notes often mean one thing—someone is after money. Therefore, you must consider that the motive behind the pup-napping might be financial. I asked for a recent photograph of Dave.

EVIDENCE LOG 3.

Dave, the teacup
Yorkshire Terrier

I must admit, even a hardened detective like me found Dave, with his big round eyes and little nose, rather heart-melting.

"He isn't fond of anyone but me," Ivanna continued. "He normally yaps if someone he doesn't know comes near him. I'm surprised he didn't raise the alarm the moment someone approached. He has behaved quite viciously toward the mail carrier in the past."

Looking at those adorable puppy eyes, it was hard to believe that Dave had it in him to be vicious, but you must remember that appearances can be deceptive. A good detective must never be taken in, even by something so utterly adorable.

"When did you last have Dave?" I asked.

"At the village festival. I left him tied to a pole outside the tent during judging for the Largest Vegetable Competition."

"And what time was this?" I asked.

"Between 2:00 p.m. and 3:00 p.m."

"I'm going to need a list of all the people who were in attendance."

After some painstaking work, Ivanna was finally able to produce a complete record of the names of people who attended the competition.

FRED LITTLE	CAPTAIN PHILLIPS
MAVIS BOLD	SALLY PHILLIPS
FATHER BARNABY	DIANNE COLLINS
TYRONNE GRIGGS	HECTOR BROWN
GAVIN FINKLEBOTTOM	MORRIS NORRIS
BARBARA NOVAK	PETER KNOX

I told Ivanna to let me know if the pup-napper contacted her again and reassured her that I would do my very best to reunite her with Dave.

I then set about gathering statements from everyone at the festival.

This is where you take over. You will need to find which of the festival attendees doesn't have an alibi for the 2:00–3:00 p.m. time period during the Largest Vegetable Competition when Dave was stolen.

First, read the following statements to compile a timetable for the day. It's important to know what happened when, and it always helps to have an order.

MAVIS BOLD

ROLE AT FESTIVAL: MEMBER OF THE LOCAL WOMEN'S ASSOCIATION (WA)

I was part of the quilt-making demonstration that kicked off the festival. I also had a Victoria sponge entered in the Best Cake Competition. Everyone thought I should have won, but Father Barnaby chose Barbara Novak's Black Forest gateau and she's not even a churchgoer. I remember seeing dear little Dave outside the tent on my way back from the hot dog van. I was there for the rest of the day, selling bric-a-brac. I didn't even get to watch the vegetable competition in the tent and certainly had no time to steal a dog! I was on my feet all day.

TYRONNE GRIGGS

ROLE AT FESTIVAL: MEMBER OF THE PUBLIC

Didn't see any dog. Only came for the vegetable competition. I like giant vegetables. I went home straight after Father Barnaby announced Gavin Finklebottom as the winner. The win really annoyed Peter Knox. He had a sizeable squash, too, but in the end, Gavin won on weight.

FRED LITTLE

ROLE AT FESTIVAL: HOT DOG VENDOR

I couldn't have stolen Dave because I was selling hot dogs next to the tent from 9:00 a.m. to 4:00 p.m. The only time I was away from the van was when Hector Brown took over so I could enter my lemon drizzle in the cake competition at 11:30 a.m. I was almost late entering because the WA had come to refuel after their quilting demonstration.

DIANNE COLLINS

ROLE AT FESTIVAL: MEMBER OF THE WA AND COMPETITION ENTRANT

It was a rather wonderful festival for me. I very much enjoyed taking part in the quilting demo, and I took home three awards, but definitely no dog. My plum tomato got a special commendation in the vegetable competition, I won Most Interesting Flavor Combination for my peach and bacon muffins, and at the end of the day, I took the trophy home for the third year in a row for the knobbliest knees.

FATHER BARNABY

ROLE AT FESTIVAL: VILLAGE VICAR AND
JUDGE OF NUMEROUS COMPETITIONS

I'm afraid I didn't see anything untoward going on, but then I was incredibly busy. My first judging role was to decide who was this year's star baker. Then, I had to judge the largest vegetable. Gavin Finklebottom won with a truly tremendous squash. Unfortunately, I suffered an injury when Peter Knox accidentally poked me in the eye with his oversized butter bean. Luckily, good old Morris Norris of St. John's Ambulance was on hand to patch me up so I was able to make it on time to judge the knobbliest knees at 3:30 p.m. Well done to Dianne Collins—she has a pair of patellae a gargoyle would be proud of!

ROLE AT FESTIVAL: ST. JOHN'S AMBULANCE
VOLUNTEER

You might think that a village festival is relatively
risk free — but think again. I had three injuries to
deal with that Sunday. The first was a blow to the
head. It happened only half an hour after the festival
opened. Sally Phillips clocked poor Captain Phillips
right on the head when she was trying to bash the
ferret — Little Dumpleton's version of Whack-a-Mole.
He was quite delirious — I sent them straight home.
That was the end of the festival for them, which
annoyed Sally because she felt sure of a win with
her Battenberg in the cake competition.

After that, Barbara Novak came with a scalded
mouth. Apparently, she was incredibly hungry after
her quilting and bit into her hot dog before it had a
chance to cool. That thing must have reached volcanic
temperatures because the size of that blister — it was a
doozy! End of the day for her, too.

Following Barbara, I saw the vicar — he'd taken a
butter bean to the eyeball. It was when I was patching
him up that I first heard Dave had gone missing. So, as
you can see, I was busy all day, I didn't have the time
for any dog-napping.

HECTOR BROWN

ROLE AT FESTIVAL: HANDYMAN

I was at the festival all day: I helped put up the tent in the morning, then took it down again at the end of the night. It was touch and go as to whether I'd have it up in time for the WA, and Mavis Bold was getting quite fretful—but Hector Brown never lets you down! I stayed to watch the quilting demonstration as I don't mind a bit of sewing myself—find it quite therapeutic. I had to leave before they finished, as I realized I'd left my tools out. Shame I didn't get to stay longer. Then I went to cover for Fred at the the hot dog stand so he could go enter his lemon drizzle in the bake-off. I'm afraid there was a slight accident when Barbara bit into a hot dog: I told her it was hot, but I don't think her hearing aid was turned up.

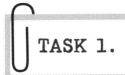

TASK 1.

Well, it was quite a day at the festival, wasn't it, my young detective? From these initial witness statements, you should be able to work out a running order of events for the day.

KNOBBLIEST KNEES COMPETITION

BEST CAKE COMPETITION

QUILTING DEMONSTRATION

LARGEST VEGETABLE COMPETITION

9:00 A.M.-10:00 A.M.	
11:30 A.M.-12:30 P.M.	
2:00 P.M.-3:00 P.M.	
3:30 P.M.-4:00 P.M.	

Answer on page 176

Now, from these witness statements you need to determine who was still at the festival at the time of the pup-napping, and who was involved in the vegetable competition. If they were occupied marveling at massive veggies inside the tent, they couldn't have been busy taking off with a teacup terrier.

Put a ✗ or ✔ in each box.

NAME	At festival at the time of the Veg Comp.	In the tent during Veg Comp.
MAVIS BOLD		
TYRONNE GRIGGS		
FRED LITTLE		
DIANNE COLLINS		
FATHER BARNABY		
MORRIS NORRIS		

Answer on page 177

Notes:

NAME	At festival at the time of the Veg Comp.	In the tent during Veg Comp.
HECTOR BROWN		
CAPTAIN PHILLIPS		
SALLY PHILLIPS		
GAVIN FINKLEBOTTOM		
PETER KNOX		
BARBARA NOVAK		

TASK 3.

So, based on this information you should have four suspects who had the opportunity to steal the charming little fluff ball that is Dave.

Write their names here:

1	
2	
3	
4	

Excellent! You are making progress!

 HARTIGAN'S HINT: Potential suspects are those at the festival at the time of the vegetable competition but not in the tent.

Answer on page 178

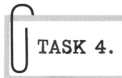

TASK 4.

The next important piece of the puzzle comes from a photograph of the crime scene. It shows the pole that Dave was tied to. From this photograph, what can you see that may have been used to subdue yappy little Dave, so he didn't raise the alarm?

EVIDENCE LOG 6.

A _ _ _   _ _ _ was used to subdue Dave.

 HARTIGAN'S HINT: Fred Little sold the item that distracted Dave.

Answer on page 178

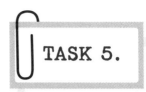

TASK 5.

Knowing what was used to keep Dave quiet, look back through the witness statements to determine which of the four suspects could have been in possession of the hot dog you spotted in the photo.

Put a ✘ or ✔ in the "In possession" box.

Name	In possession of hot dog?
MAVIS BOLD	
FRED LITTLE	
MORRIS NORRIS	
HECTOR BROWN	

Based on this information, you should have eliminated one person from your list of suspects!

Who are you eliminating? _____

Answer on page 179

TASK 6.

Now you need to deduce how the perpetrator managed to cut Dave's leash. Once you have read the evidence, fill in the chart on the next page. We are looking for a blade that would leave a neat zigzag cut.

EVIDENCE LOG 7.

- Hector Brown was seen using a handsaw to help him put up the tent.

- Cake knives were handled by Father Barnaby, Mavis Bold, Fred Little, and Dianne Collins.

- Fred Little and Hector Brown each used a kitchen knife to cut apart strings of sausages.

- All the ladies of the WA used pinking shears to cut quilt squares during their demonstration.

- Morris Norris has angled shears in his medical bag to cut bandages.

- Gavin Finklebottom was seen using gardening clippers to cut the twine that he used to keep his enormous squash in place.

29

Based on what you know about who had access to which tools, write the appropriate name (or names) under each item.

HANDSAW	CAKE KNIFE	KITCHEN KNIFE

Answer on page 180

PINKING SHEARS	ANGLED SHEARS	GARDEN CLIPPERS

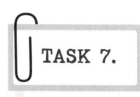

TASK 7.

It is accusation time! You should be able to deduce from your final three suspects who had the blade that cut Dave's leash.

Cluedunnit? Make your accusation here:

_____

_____

HARTIGAN'S HINT: Think about what the resulting cut from each blade would look like.

Detective notes:

Mavis Bold! Jolly good show, super sleuth! You wouldn't have suspected a person of such standing to be involved in pupnapping, which is why it is important for a detective to always keep an open mind.

Mavis was at the festival at the time but not watching the vegetable competition so had opportunity. She also visited the hot dog stand with the other WA ladies! Her pinking shears are the only blade that could leave the neat zigzag cut we saw in the evidence photo of the leash.

So, why did she do it? It seems most out of character. As is often the case, one crime will lead to another. I think you need to dig a little deeper, Detective. And so onward to **Case 2: Misbehaving Mavis**.

Notes and deductions:

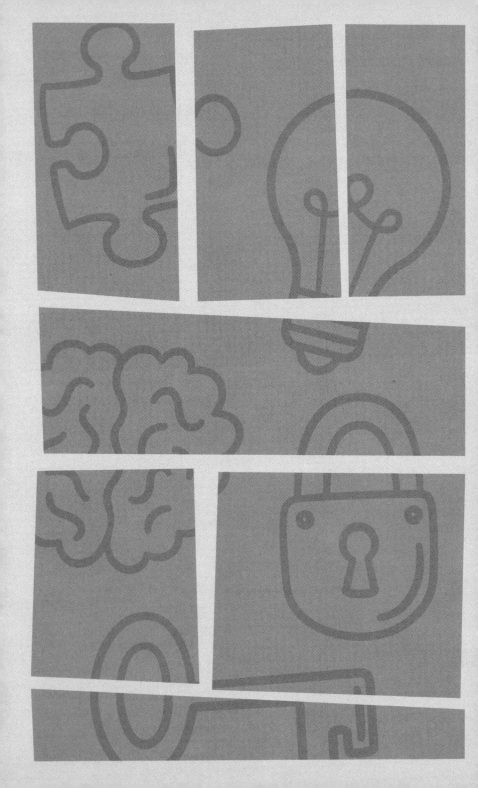

CASE 2:
MISBEHAVING MAVIS

U nder the staggering weight of your evidence, Mavis immediately buckled and confessed to stealing Dave. She returned the pup to a grateful Ivanna soon after the confession. The reason for her crime, however, remains a mystery—one which I am confident you can solve!

Here is a transcript of her confession to the police. I'm afraid it is not a lot to go on.

EVIDENCE LOG 1.

"I had to do it. I didn't mean Dave any harm. In fact, he very much enjoyed his time with me watching reruns of *Doctor Who*. But I had every intention of giving him back. *Once* Ivanna had given me what I wanted."

Mavis babbled incoherently a bit about an alibi, an apology, and some money, but became tight-lipped after that. She seemed quite nervous when pressed. A search of Mavis's bag uncovered a note addressed to her.

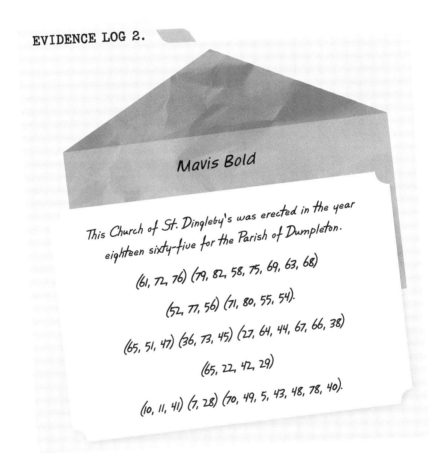

Mavis Bold

This Church of St. Dingleby's was erected in the year eighteen sixty-five for the Parish of Dumpleton.

(61, 72, 76) (79, 82, 58, 75, 69, 63, 68)

(52, 77, 56) (71, 80, 55, 54).

(65, 51, 47) (36, 73, 45) (27, 64, 44, 67, 66, 38)

(65, 22, 42, 29)

(10, 11, 41) (7, 28) (70, 49, 5, 43, 48, 78, 40).

Rather baffling, don't you think? Why would anyone write to tell Mavis when St. Dingleby's was erected? The numbers below the message about the church must be some sort of code. You'll need to crack it to determine what it says.

TASK 1.

On the back of the note there is a cipher grid. If you complete it, you should be able to replace the numbers in brackets with letters. Perhaps the message about St. Dingleby's will help you fill out the grid.

Write the message to Mavis in the grid—one letter per box, no spaces or punctuation. Then, add the remaining numbers to the grid.

	H	I	S				R		
82	81	80	79			76			73
			T						
	71	70	69				65		
	Y								
	61								
T	E	D	I						
							45	44	43
									N
					37	36			33
					F	I	V	E	F
	31		29						23
O	R								
	21	20	19	18	17				
				U	M	P			T
				8					
O									
2	1								

Answer on page 181–182

HARTIGAN'S HINT: The numbers descend backward in the grid from 82–1.

What did the note say? Write your findings here:

_____

_____

_____

_____

It looks like someone is blackmailing Mavis Bold!

Whoever wrote the note appears to believe that Mavis is responsible for a fire and Mavis was willing to pup-nap Dave as ransom to keep them quiet! But what has this got to do with a flying goat? And not just *a* flying goat, but *the* flying goat!

Detective notes:

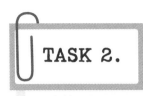

TASK 2.

Mavis is no longer talking, but we need to deduce what "the flying goat" refers to. To discover what Mavis wanted from Ivanna, find out which listed word is **missing** from the word search below. (Often, as a detective, you need to be attuned not only to what is there in front of you, but also what is not!) The words may appear forward, backward, up, down, or diagonally.

ALIBI	JEWELS	PROPERTY
APOLOGY	KEYS	SOLVE
CONFESSION	MONEY	STATUE
CONTRACT	PAINTING	VASE

```
E  C  O  N  T  R  A  C  T  N  V  C
V  Z  N  K  E  F  U  O  W  R  E  J
L  O  E  F  S  M  O  N  E  Y  O  M
O  Y  X  E  E  S  S  F  H  W  P  L
S  R  B  M  V  A  S  E  L  E  R  Y
O  O  S  P  M  L  T  S  F  E  O  F
S  Q  S  R  E  I  A  S  S  Z  P  G
Z  U  O  W  E  B  T  I  A  B  E  N
L  I  E  N  Z  I  U  O  I  P  R  S
S  J  P  W  A  T  E  N  A  O  T  F
O  O  Z  O  A  P  O  L  O  G  Y  W
T  U  P  E  W  Z  O  E  E  P  K  E
```

The missing item that Mavis wanted is:

_____

Could that be what *The Flying Goat* is? That may explain
why Mavis tried to pup-nap Dave from Ivanna. After all,
Ivanna is the owner of the local art gallery, so she would
have access to any piece of art that Mavis may be after.

Answers on page 183

I believe it is time to check the village records to determine why Mavis is being blackmailed! Perhaps the *Dumpleton Daily* newspaper archive can shed some light on this fire.

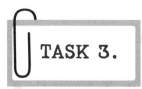

TASK 3.

To unlock the news archives, you will need to enter a four-digit passcode. The four digits will be shown in the shaded squares of this 6 × 6 puzzle. To solve this puzzle, you must write in numbers 1–6 so that they appear only once in each row, column, and block.

 HARTIGAN'S HINT: In each 3 × 2 block, the numbers 1–6 can only appear once.

1	2	3
4	5	6

1		3			
	6	2			
3		6	5		2
			1	6	3
5	2	1	6	3	
		4			5

Read the numbers in the shaded boxes from top to bottom.

Enter the passcode here:

Answer on page 184

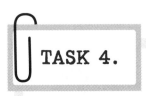

Nice investigating! You have unlocked the *Dumpleton Daily* records. You select news articles filed under **F** for FIRE.

Index Number	
FA001	
FA002	
FE001	
FI001	
FI002	
FI003	
FL001	
FR002	

Below is an index of news stories returned by your search.
Which stories are of interest to you? Circle the index numbers.

Article Description
Fascinating Find! A maze used for ferret racing has been unearthed in the fields at the back of Captain Phillips's house . . .
Father Barnaby Cries Holy Smoke! St. Dingleby's church, the heart of Little Dumpleton, has suffered a terrible fire . . .
Fenced In! Firefighters called out after Fred Little gets head stuck in the railings around the village pond. Villagers are being advised to proceed with caution when feeding the ducks.
Fight breaks out during hotly contested lawn bowling tournament, leaving two members of the WA concussed and one mobility vehicle submerged in the village pond . . .
Finger Bun Inferno at Brilliant Buns . . .
Finklebottom blames hungry badgers for the loss of his turnip crop . . .
Flaming Fiasco: A Hair-Raising Episode at Tyronne's Trims!
Fred Little's frightful discovery as he realized he has been posting his letter in the dog waste bin for two years . . .

Answer on page 185

From your research, you determine that there have been three significant fires. Time to take a closer look.

THE
DUMPLETON DAILY

FINGER BUN INFERNO!

A blaze at Dianne Collins's bakery, Brilliant Buns, was very swiftly brought under control by a local man.

A batch of finger buns caught fire after Dianne forgot she had put them in the oven and left them there for seventy hours.

Hector Brown happened to be passing when he saw a fire through the window of the closed shop.

Heroically, he put out the flames before any real damage could be done. He received two dozen fresh doughnuts as a reward.

FLAMING FIASCO: A HAIR-RAISING EPISODE AT TYRONNE'S TRIMS!

Barbara Novak received quite a fright after a helmet-style hair dryer exploded and caught fire on her head.

Quick-thinking Tyronne Griggs immediately put out the fire with a fire extinguisher.

The flames left little permanent damage (aside from the damage to Barbara's perm).

Tyronne is offering 50 percent off perms for the foreseeable future.

FATHER BARNABY CRIES HOLY SMOKE!

St. Dingleby's church, the heart of Little Dumpleton, has suffered a terrible fire.

It is still not known how the blaze started but there is some suggestion that a candle may have set light to the quilt that was donated to the church by the Women's Association.

The beloved quilt, depicting Saint Coltide—the patron saint of disappointed children—which hung from one of the rafters, appears to have caused the flames to spread rapidly to the roof.

The fire was discovered by Father Barnaby and Mavis Bold, who is responsible for the church flower arrangements and was a contributor to the aforementioned quilt. Bold said, "I honestly have no idea how it happened."

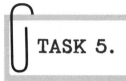

TASK 5.

Which of the three news stories, A, B, or C, do you think is relevant to Mavis Bold's case? _____

This is certainly an interesting finding, but we have yet to discover why Mavis was blackmailed to "Get *The Flying Goat*" specifically. What is it about that painting? When you find out, present your discoveries to Mavis—perhaps she will be more forthcoming with information once she knows you are onto her!

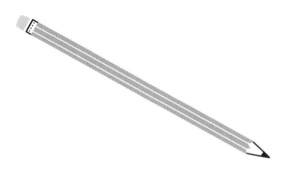

Answer on page 185

Deductions so far:

TASK 6.

Solve the crossword puzzle, then rearrange the letters in the gray squares to discover the secret of *The Flying Goat*.

ACROSS

2. What object may have caused the fire at the church?
5. What sort of children is St. Coltide the patron saint of?
6. What type of buns caught on fire?

DOWN

1. What hairdo was Barbara getting?
3. What did Hector receive as a reward?
4. Who owns the hair salon?

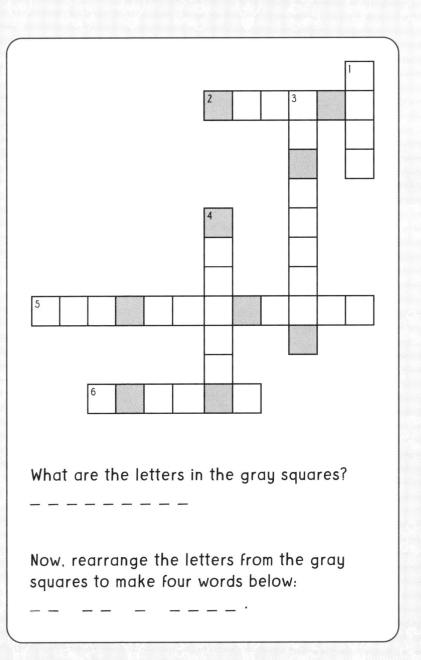

What are the letters in the gray squares?

_ _ _ _ _ _ _ _ _

Now, rearrange the letters from the gray
squares to make four words below:

_ _   _ _   _   _ _ _ _ .

Answer on page 186

Excellent work, detective! *The Flying Goat* is a clue of some sort. But a clue to what? That will require more investigation.

When you presented your findings to Mavis, she did indeed admit to starting the fire in St. Dingleby's, though she said it was an accident. Apparently, she was listening to music on her headphones and dancing about as she arranged the flowers that fateful evening. She did not realize she had knocked a candle over with a flailing limb until it was too late, and alas, by that point the fire had spread. Someone else must know she was responsible. The very person blackmailing her. Who that is, Mavis either did not know or would not say. Nor did she have any idea as to why they wanted the painting *The Flying Goat*.

Which means, my dear detective, we must commence **Case 3: The Mystery of The Flying Goat**.

Write yourself a reminder of the key
pieces of evidence and people involved
so far.

Who:

What:

Where:

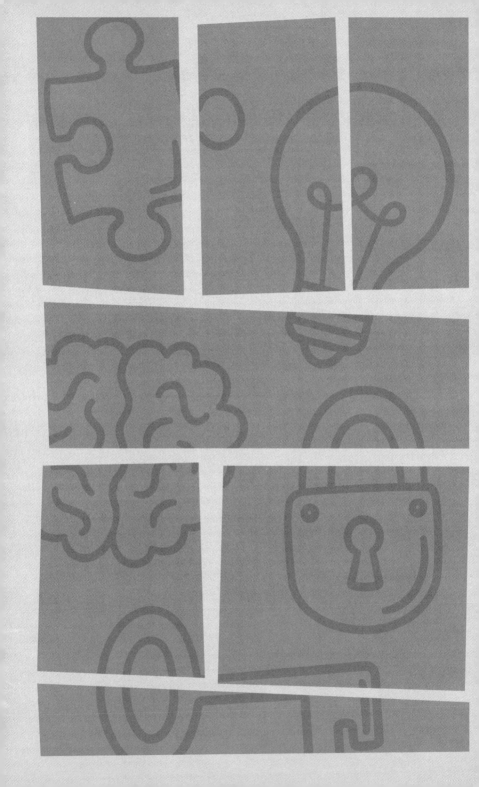

CASE 3:
THE MYSTERY OF
THE FLYING GOAT

F or this case, it is important to determine why *The Flying Goat* is of such value to the blackmailer, and hopefully, this will lead you to uncover their identity. Perhaps it is a painting of exceptional artistic worth and beauty? Maybe it is a rare artwork from a famous painter and has an eye-wateringly expensive price tag?

Whatever it is, it is essential that you examine it to see whether you can discover its secret. So, off you go to the local art gallery, for more sleuthing.

The gallery is locked when you get there. You call Ivanna, thinking she may be able to let you in, but she doesn't answer her phone. Her voicemail message informs you that she has gone away for some quality time with Dave at a pet grooming spa to help them process the trauma of the pup-napping. You realize that the art gallery will be closed until she gets back. However, stopping in the middle of investigating a lead is out of the question. You will have to find your own way in. Entering the gallery for investigative purposes is technically breaking and entering, but given the circumstances, I'm sure Ivanna would understand.

You examine the outside of the art gallery, inelegantly named The Drawing Dump, and find that all the windows are firmly shut. You try to reach the lock on the inside of the door by putting your arm through the letter box, but frustratingly, your arms are not long enough. However, there is a number lock on the door that you might be able to open.

You're going to have to crack the code to open the door.

There are four shapes on the door handle. You deduce that the shapes must have something to do with the code. Above the handle on the door is a small metal etching.

On closer inspection, you see it is a reproduction of an artwork, and when you look closer still, you see that there are shapes on it that match the ones on the handle! You have a hunch that if you count the shapes, it may give you the code for the door. But, even with your sharp eyes, the plaque is far too small for you to count the shapes accurately. You peer through the window and see several pieces of artwork on the wall. Three of them look very much like the one etched on the door handle. But which one will tell you the code?

 HARTIGAN'S HINT: Which picture only contains the shapes you see on the door handle?

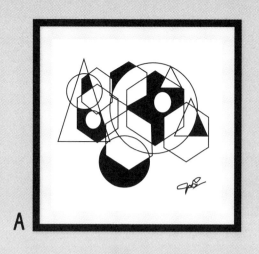

A

B

C

Answer on page 187

Excellent! You've identified the correct painting. Now look at the painting below and count the shapes.

Once you've counted how many of each shape there are, write the numbers in the correct order in the spaces under the door handle to unlock the door.

Enter your code here:

 HARTIGAN'S HINT: Shapes may be rotated or stretched.

Answer on page 188

Fabulous work! You step inside, feeling a little pleased with yourself, but immediately realize there is a problem. The Drawing Dump has a state-of-the-art laser-beam security system. You must not get caught in the lasers or the alarm will go off—you cannot afford any costly time delays that would occur if you had to explain your actions to the police. You will have to find a route through that does not trigger the lasers.

Your first stop will be Ivanna's desk, to see if you can find any information that will help with your investigation. It might prove useful to find out who has visited the art gallery recently, as they may have been interested in *The Flying Goat*.

Notes:

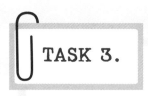

TASK 3.

Find the path through to the desk without triggering the lasers.

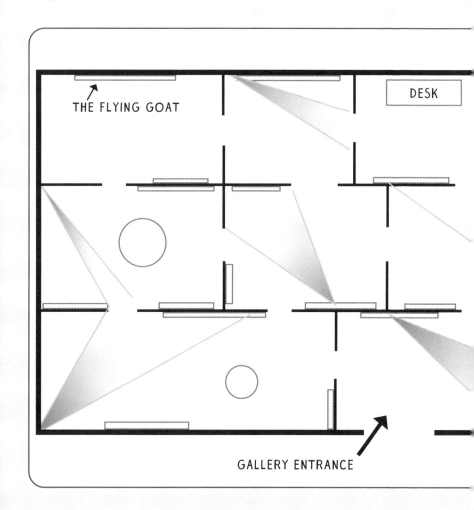

THE FLYING GOAT

DESK

GALLERY ENTRANCE

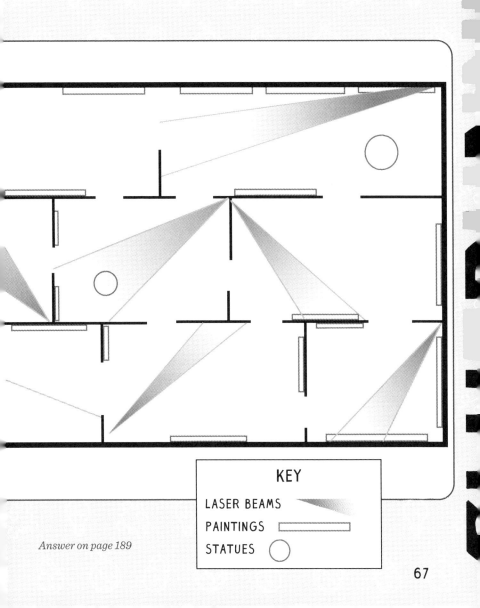

KEY

LASER BEAMS

PAINTINGS

STATUES

Answer on page 189

Well done—you remained composed and made it to Ivanna's desk. You spot her laptop but see it is password protected. You look around for any clues as to what the password might be. Sometimes people make the mistake of writing their passwords down in case they forget them. I once discovered the codes to a bank vault thanks to a cleaner named Boris who had taped the codes to the end of his broom. Unfortunately, Ivanna has been more careful.

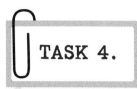

TASK 4.

You'll need to try to reset the password instead. This will probably be a breeze for you—I hear the youth of today are exceedingly tech savvy.

The computer asks you to answer two security questions to reset the password. You're going to have to use what you know about Ivanna to answer the questions.

RESET USER PASSWORD

Answer the following questions:

Question 1: What is the name of your first pet?

Answer: _ _ _ _

Question 2: What was your favorite subject in school?

Answer: _ _ _

HARTIGAN'S HINT:
Question 1: Who has been pup-napped?
Question 2: Where are you now?

Answer on page 190

You guess correctly, reset her password, and you're in! It might be nice to write it down for her, so when she returns from her pup-grooming, she's not locked out. A good detective is a considerate detective.

You open the file that says *customers* and bring up a list of the most recent visitors to the gallery.

EVIDENCE LOG 1.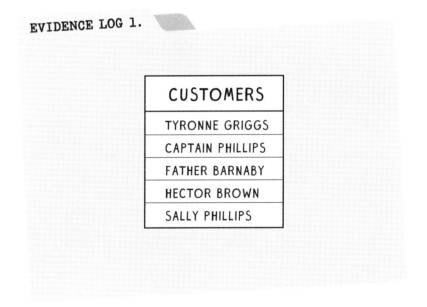

CUSTOMERS
TYRONNE GRIGGS
CAPTAIN PHILLIPS
FATHER BARNABY
HECTOR BROWN
SALLY PHILLIPS

Take note, as this may be important later in your investigation. Now you need to take a closer look at *The Flying Goat*.

You spot it on a far wall, hidden away in the corner, possibly for good reason. You make your way back through the laser beams, following the course you have already mapped out.

You arrive at the painting, and the hypothesis that *The Flying Goat* might be a painting of exceptional artistic worth and beauty is disproven immediately. It is quite . . . something. I suppose you could call it modern art. Or you could call it an assault to the eyes, which is possibly more accurate.

Many great artists, such as Leonardo da Vinci, Hieronymus Bosch, and Frida Kahlo, to name a few, are believed to have included hidden meanings in their work. Perhaps Basil van Goof, the artist who painted *The Flying Goat*, has hidden a message in his.

TASK 5.

There *is* a secret message hidden in the painting. Can you work out what it is? Pay particular attention to letters that are linked to others.

Write your answer here: _ _ _ _   _ _ _ _

 HARTIGAN'S HINT: Arrange the letters connected to GOAT GOAT to make two new words.

Answer on page 191

Notes:

Aha! I knew that wouldn't stump you! There it is—a map on the back of the painting. What could it be—a treasure map? There's also a poem that contains instructions.

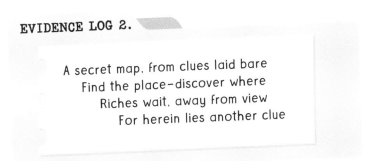

EVIDENCE LOG 2.

A secret map, from clues laid bare
Find the place—discover where
Riches wait, away from view
For herein lies another clue

LITTLE DUMPLETON

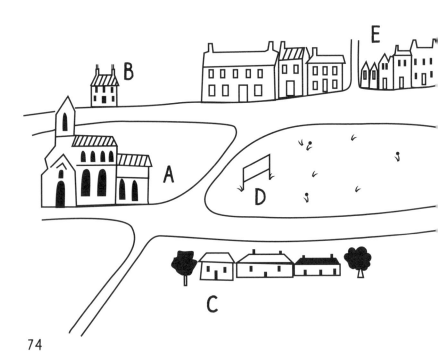

A St. Dingleby's Church
B Office Building
C Cottages
D Village Green
E Bakery
F Dumpleton Manor
G Hotel
H Dumpleton Farm
I Playground
J Monument
K Pond
L Post Office
M Coffee Shop

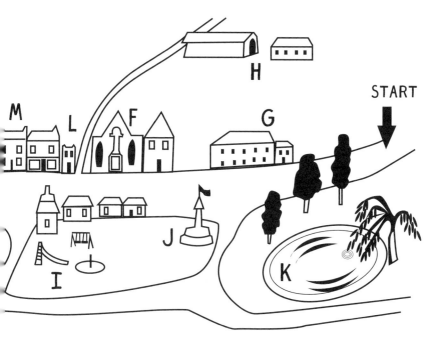

START

M L F G

H

J

K

I

 HARTIGAN'S HINT: There is a map on the next page with hoof guidelines if you need help. Remember to look for the correct starting hoof and pay attention to the compass!

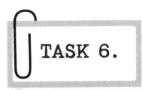

TASK 6.

Work out how many hoofprints to move forward by following the clues in the instructions. Make sure you use the compass.

- **N** is the ___ letter in **A**. Go slightly **AT** this number of paces.

- You should be at a village site. The second **N** is the ___ letter in **J**. Go **T** this number of paces.

A St. Dingleby's Church
B Office Building
C Cottages
D Village Green
E Bakery
F Dumpleton Manor
G Hotel

H Dumpleton Farm
I Playground
J Monument
K Pond
L Post Office
M Coffee Shop

- From here, if you look **GO** along the side street you should see an important milk producer for the village. **O** in this landmark is the ___ letter. Go **T** this number of paces.

- **N** is the ___ letter in **K**. Go **AT** this number of paces.

- You should find yourself between two landmarks. The landmark to your **T** is the final destination.

Where are you? Write your answer here:

It's time for you to head to that location and have a snoop around to see what you can discover.

KEY
Size of one pace

H

START

M

L

F

G

J

I

K

LITTLE DUMPLETON

Answer on page 192

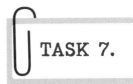

There are three headstones in front of St. Dingleby's church. One of them is of interest to your case. Which one? There may be a clue in the poem you found on the back of *The Flying Goat.*

A

IN MEMORY
OF
ALICE
COLLINS

1794 – 1881

WHO DISCOVERED
SHE COULD
NOT SWIM

MAY SHE
REST IN PEACE

FOREVER LOVED

Answer on page 194

The correct gravestone is _____ _____.

 HARTIGAN'S HINT: Look at the poem you found with the map on page 74. What do you notice about the letters that start each line? Can you see a connection with one of the gravestones?

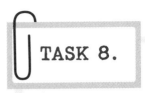

TASK 8.

Before you start digging up graves looking for treasure, take a closer look at that tombstone.

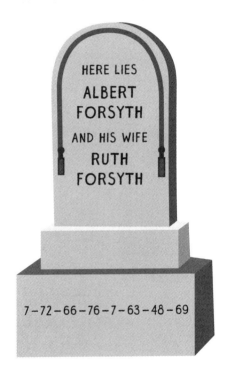

HERE LIES
ALBERT FORSYTH
AND HIS WIFE
RUTH FORSYTH

7 – 72 – 66 – 76 – 7 – 63 – 48 – 69

There's another code to crack. Can you see it? Use the grid you already completed on page 39 when you solved Mavis's note in Case 2!

Where should we head next?

– – – – – – –

Answer on page 195

When you arrive, it looks as if someone has already been here. The little door at the back is ajar! When you look inside, there's a small chest, but the lid is open, and it is empty. Whatever was in the chest has been taken. But by whom?

Time to look for witnesses. You spot Gavin Finklebottom carrying his enormous squash toward the farmers' market and Dianne Collins heading off to the post office.

When you ask them if they saw anyone leaving, Gavin confirms that he did. He can tell you what color shoes and pants they were wearing but says that he couldn't see much more because his squash—that he tells you he has inexplicably named Marvin—was blocking his view. Dianne, who had just left The Fidgety Fox (the village coffee shop) for the post office, says she saw three people in the vicinity. They were Hector Brown, Father Barnaby, and Captain Phillips. When you ask if they were wearing different pants, she says, "They'd hardly all fit in the same pair now, would they?" This is a fair point and highlights the importance of asking clear questions. You rephrase and she confirms they were indeed all wearing different types of pants and different colored shoes. You then take six further statements from her regarding their attire. Hopefully, you will be able to determine who was wearing what and compare that to Gavin's description of the person he saw leaving the monument.

TASK 9.

To work out who was wearing what, you will need to use your powers of elimination. Read Dianne's slightly garbled witness statements below and complete the grid.

1. The person wearing chinos was not wearing green shoes.

2. Hector doesn't own a suit and wasn't wearing brown shoes.

3. Captain Phillips would never wear jeans and wasn't wearing black shoes.

4. Hector was either wearing jeans *or* brown shoes with chinos.

5. If Hector was wearing jeans. Captain Phillips wasn't wearing a suit.

6. Whoever was wearing the suit was also wearing black shoes.

Answer on page 196

To solve this, place an ✘ where a statement isn't true and a ✔ if it is correct. Number 1 has been done for you.

		Shoe color			Pants worn		
		BROWN	GREEN	BLACK	JEANS	CHINOS	SUIT
Suspects	HECTOR						
	BARNABY						
	CAPTAIN P.						
Pants worn	JEANS						
	CHINOS		✘				
	SUIT						

HARTIGAN'S HINT: If a suspect's name *is* mentioned in the statement, put a check or an X in the row along from their name. If the suspect's name isn't mentioned in the statement, use the bottom section of the grid where the suspects' names aren't listed.

TASK 10.

Draw your conclusions.

Gavin says that the person he could see coming out of the monument was wearing chinos and brown shoes.

Who did Gavin see?

_____

_____

If Father Barnaby lives in the cottages, Hector Brown lives at Dumpleton Farm, and Captain Phillips lives at Dumpleton Manor . . .

Where should you head next to continue your investigation?

_____

_____

Excellent! Onward, to **Case 4: Furblast**.

Answer on page 196

Make a note of key pieces of evidence
and possible culprits below:

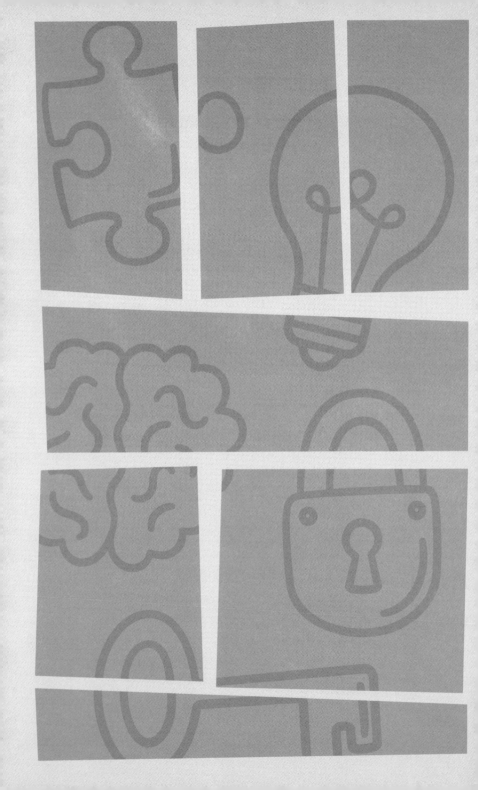

CASE 4:
FURBLAST

It is clear Captain Phillips is somehow involved in the case. What else could explain his presence at the monument? Was he the one blackmailing Mavis for the painting? Did he discover its secrets for himself? He was on Ivanna's list of people who visited the art gallery. What did he find in the monument? It must be something of value. Whatever is happening, it is clear that you need to interrogate the Captain. Hopefully you will find some answers at Dumpleton Manor.

When you arrive at the Captain's home, his wife, Sally Phillips, flings open the door before you can even ring the bell. She is wearing a dressing gown, her hair is full of rollers, and she is wielding a large baseball bat in a somewhat threatening manner.

She is rather startling, but you hold your nerve and just about resist the urge to scream. You don't have to be a detective to tell by the look on her face that something is wrong.

"There's been a robbery. I thought they might have returned," she says, lowering the baseball bat. "They broke in through the back door. I was upstairs getting ready, so I don't know exactly when it happened."

You ask if you can take a look, and she leads you to the back door. Sure enough, there are signs of a forced entry. What on earth is going on? You thought the Captain might be involved in criminal activity, but it seems that he might also be a victim!

Sally tells you that nothing was taken from the house, but the spare keys from the hooks by the back door have been tampered with. She thinks that one of them might be missing.

You step outside to look for any further clues and see that there are several sets of footprints by the back door. One set could belong to whomever broke in.

You count five separate pairs of footprints and label them A–E. Sally tells you that no one else has been out the back door other than herself and her husband. If you compare the footprints to her shoes and the Captain's shoes, you may see evidence that could incriminate the person who broke in.

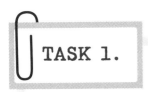

TASK 1.

These are Sally and Captain Phillips's shoes and the footprints they make.

Sally Phillips's footwear	Captain Phillips's footwear

Answer on page 197

These are the footprints that were left in the mud. You need to work out which of the five sets of footprints belong to Sally and Captain Phillips and which could belong to the suspect. Circle the suspect's footprints.

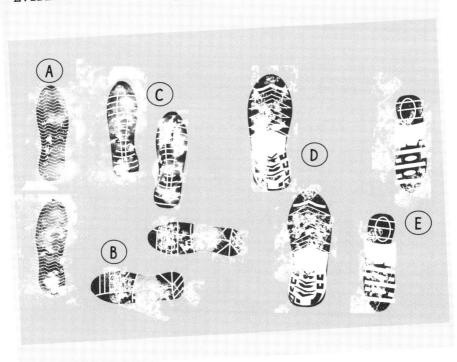

You now ask Sally about the missing key. She reasserts that one has been taken. Luckily, she has her set to use as a comparison. If there is a key missing from the ones hanging at the back door, you will know for certain, and Sally will be able to tell you what that key unlocks.

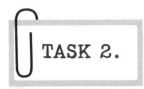

TASK 2.

Can you figure out which key is missing? Circle the key in Sally's set that is missing from the keys that were left on the hooks at the back door.

Sally's set of keys:

Answer on page 198

EVIDENCE LOG 2.

Keys left at the back door:

Well done! You identified which key is missing. Sally tells you it is the key to the back door of Captain Phillips's office building. Apparently, he told her he was heading there earlier today.

Perhaps he went there after he went to the monument? Whoever stole the Captain's key may be at his office, too! Could the Captain be in danger?

Supersleuth, you know where you need to go! Sally lets you hold on to the key as evidence.

When you arrive at Captain Phillips's office, it is all locked up. You can hear muffled noises from inside. You use the key to unlock the door, then cautiously open it and find the Captain tied to a chair with a bucket over his head! It does not take a genius to realize that he did not do this to himself. You remove the bucket and discover that someone has stuffed a sock in his mouth. You wonder if it could be evidence. Perhaps the sock belongs to whoever has tied up the Captain, but then you see that the Captain has one bare foot and realize the sock must be his.

You remove the sock, but don't untie him just yet—it might be useful to keep him where he is while you question him.

He tells you he's been attacked, but when you ask him who did it, he says he doesn't know. Whoever it was attacked from behind and Captain Phillips was unconscious when they tied him up.

This blows your case wide open!

When you ask him if this has anything to do with what he found in the monument, he looks shocked.

"How could you possibly know about that? The Dumpleton Diamond is a secret. Very few people know it even exists."

The Dumpleton Diamond! So, the map on the back of *The Flying Goat* painting was a treasure map after all—a treasure map to the Dumpleton Diamond! That must have been what was inside the monument.

You try not to show your excitement at this bombshell and press him to tell you a little more about this Dumpleton Diamond.

"It is a family heirloom. An heirloom that my great-great-grandfather Ernest was cheated out of during a game of ferret maze runner, and I finally have the evidence to prove it! Evidence that proves I am the rightful owner."

It takes you a moment to process this information. You're not quite certain what to ask about first, but settle on the ferret maze runner part of his statement.

"My great-great-grandfather, Ernest, had the fastest ferret in all of Little Dumpleton. Furblast had never been beaten. Ferret racing was a popular pastime back in his day—they'd put two ferrets into a maze to see which one would make it out of the exit first. Furblast had the best nose and the fastest paws for miles around."

Though it's hard to see where this is going, you let Captain Phillips continue.

"One day, the owner of a ferret named Bandit challenged my great-great-grandfather to a ferret maze run. The man did not give his name, but the bet was huge—if Furblast won, Ernest would get half the land in Dumpleton and a fine house in the village of Pucklebury. If he didn't, he would have to hand over the Dumpleton Diamond. He took the bet, safe in the knowledge that Furblast was a sure winner."

Captain Phillips nods over toward his desk. "In the top drawer you will find the evidence that proves that Bandit's owner was a cheat."

You open the drawer and discover a newspaper article from the *Dumpleton Daily*, detailing the ferret maze that was found.

"The photo in the article shows that there were two entrances to the maze, but the one Furblast entered had no possible route through to the finish."

Find both Bandit's and Furblast's paths to the finish.
You need to work out whether the Captain is telling
the truth.

Was it possible for Furblast to win the race?

☐ Yes   ☐ No

Answer on page 199

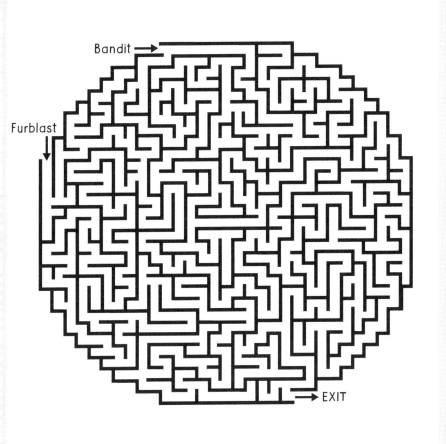

If this ferret maze map is indeed correct, it would appear that Captain Phillips may have a claim to the Dumpleton Diamond. You take the maze as evidence.

"My great-great-grandfather Ernest knew he'd been cheated," Captain Phillips continues, "so when he handed the diamond over to the unnamed stranger, he placed it in a locked chest so it could never be opened. Then we heard nothing of it, until my father, Harold Phillips, quite by accident, found a map folded inside a book he'd bought in a secondhand bookshop. He'd just joined the local lawn bowling league and bought some sort of playing guide. He couldn't believe it when the map fell from between its pages. He guessed from the poem that it may be linked to the Dumpleton Diamond, and he tried, without success, for years to figure out the instructions."

When you put the suggestion to Captain Phillips that he was blackmailing Mavis Bold to get the painting, he laughs. He only recently discovered his father had commissioned the painting as a way to hide the map. Captain Phillips knew his father had once found the map, but he'd believed it to be lost. He had thought that when, on his deathbed, his father had said, "Keep the goat," he had been referring to his great-aunt Mildred, who lived with him at the time. After his father's passing, the Captain had given *The Flying Goat* painting to the art gallery for free because he believed it to be a visual monstrosity. But he tells you that he had recently found his father's diaries, and the importance of *The Flying Goat* had become clear.

"I went to look at the painting where it hangs at The Drawing Dump. I turned it over when Ivanna wasn't watching and took a photo."

He asks you to untie him so he can take something from his back pocket. You do, and he takes out a small leather-bound book and hands it to you. It is his father's diary. "Everything I've told you will be in there."

The diary has a lock on it. Captain Phillips tells you the key is in the same drawer where you found the ferret maze. There are five keys in the drawer, but he can't remember which one opens the lock. You'll have to figure it out.

Which number key will open the lock? Circle the correct one.

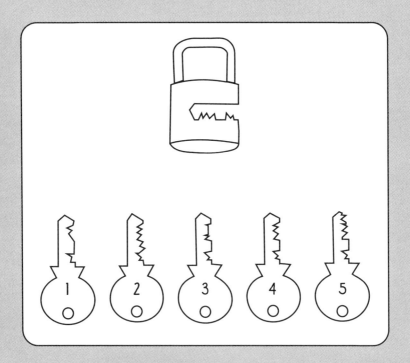

Answer on page 200

You're in! And, sure enough, the diary confirms what Captain Phillips said. There is mention of how his father found the map, and how he had hidden it behind the painting. There is something else, too, in Harold Phillips's diary that piques your detective senses—some drawings of the phases of the moon. But they aren't in order and some of them don't look correct at all. You copy them down in case they are important later.

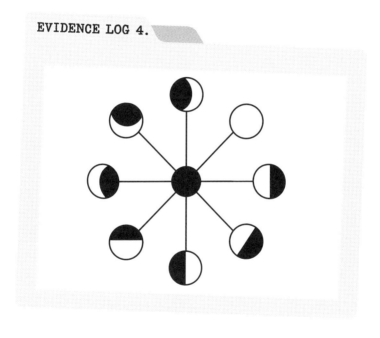

EVIDENCE LOG 4.

There's also a note written below the diagram. You copy down the contents of the note, too, even though it doesn't make much sense.

> Everything starts with a New Moon.
> Crescents wax, then quarter.
> Then crescents wane and quarter.
> Always in that order.

The Dumpleton Diamond is no longer in Captain Phillips's office, so whoever knocked him unconscious must have taken it. Captain Phillips informs you that he has security cameras installed outside. If you can access the camera footage, you may be able to catch your villain red-handed.

The only problem is that there is an access code to log in to the camera, and the knock on the head has caused Captain Phillips to forget what it is. He does have a backup method for finding out the code, and something tells me you're just the detective to figure it out. It's another maze—though there are no ferrets involved this time.

TASK 5.

Find your way to the end of the maze. The numbers that are on the correct route, in the order you pass through them, are the access code to the surveillance cameras. It could be tricky, so try it in pencil first!

Write the code here:

Answer on page 201

105

Congratulations! You have successfully gained access to the camera footage. There were three people outside Captain Phillips's office during the time period when the Captain could have been attacked: They were Hector Brown, Tyronne Griggs, and Father Barnaby.

They are now your leads for **Case 5: Partially There**.

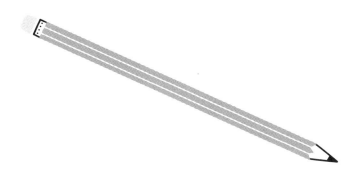

Make a note of your deductions here:

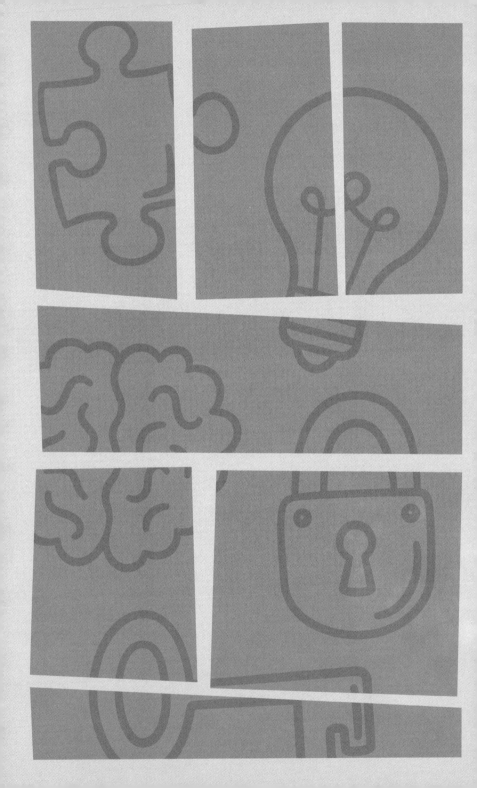

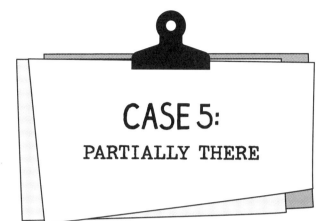

CASE 5:
PARTIALLY THERE

It would seem Father Barnaby, Hector Brown, and Tyronne Griggs are all under consideration for blackmailing Mavis and attacking Captain Phillips.

Whoever is responsible must know about *The Flying Goat*. Check your Evidence Log from Case 3 on page 70 to see whether any of these three suspects could have seen the map on the back of *The Flying Goat*.

Can you rule out anyone? _____

With this in mind, it is time to question your suspects and find out whether they have an alibi.

You send Captain Phillips to the doctor's office to get checked out and then head into the village. Mavis Bold comes rushing up to you in a fluster. She says Sally Phillips

Answer on page 202

told her about the robbery and wants to know whether you are any closer to catching the blackmailer. You tell her you are closing in. She hands you something.

"I wondered if this might be of any use. It's the envelope the coded message came in."

You take it because you know it could be useful. The blackmailer has written Mavis's name on the front. Maybe they've tried to alter their handwriting, but there may be a telltale sign that could help your investigation.

EVIDENCE LOG 1.

Writing on envelope: *Mavis Bold*

HANDWRITING SAMPLES

Father Barnaby: *Psalm 23*

Hector Brown: *$1.29/lb. spuds*

Tyronne Griggs: *Short back n sides* $15.00

 HARTIGAN'S HINT: Which letter has been used in all three handwriting samples *and* on the envelope?

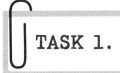

TASK 1.

Look at the handwriting style used on the envelope.
Do any of the letters in all three handwriting samples
match the writing on the envelope?

The letter ___ in two of the handwriting samples matches the
writing on the envelope. One of the handwriting samples doesn't.
You can rule out one of the suspects.

This leaves you with:

1) _____

2) _____

Your net is really closing in now. You are down to your last two
suspects. It's time to question them.

You head to Hector Brown's farm and find him in the
cowshed. To start, you think he is with someone, but then you
realize he is actually deep in conversation with a cow he's calling
Moochelle.

You interrupt politely and ask him whether he'd been near
Captain Phillips's office. He tells you he had been near there,

Answer on page 202

but that he was only passing by. He seems genuinely shocked when you tell him about the attack. You show him the envelope and ask him if he sent Mavis Bold a blackmail letter.

"Blackmail Mavis? No! Look, I'll admit, I wrote her name on that envelope, but I had nothin' to do with what's inside or clobbering Phillips over the head."

How did Mavis's letter get into Hector Brown's possession?

"There was a slight accident with the mail carrier and my tractor," he explains. "There were letters all over the sidewalk. The envelope addressed to Mavis was completely unreadable. I opened it up, saw her name, and I said that as I was on my way into the village, I'd drop it off. I wrote out a new envelope. Couldn't make heads or tails of what that letter was about, though."

This means that the handwriting on the envelope wasn't necessarily the blackmailer's! Which means that Father Barnaby is still in the picture and Tyronne is a suspect again, too! And even though Hector says he has nothing to do with the attack on Captain Phillips, you only have his word for it. You need proof to remove him from your list of suspects.

You ask if you can see the bottom of Hector's boots to check the tread.

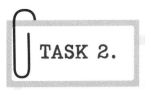

TASK 2.

Check this footprint against the footprint you have for the suspect on page 91. Does it match?

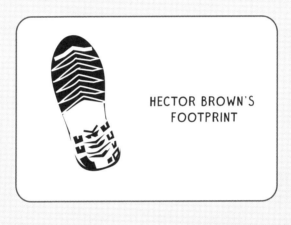

HECTOR BROWN'S
FOOTPRINT

Circle: YES/NO

You realize that you can't dismiss Hector just yet; his footprint is a match for one of the other footprints at the scene.

Whose is it? _____

Answer on page 202

This means Hector may have been there, but the prints could also be Captain Phillips's. Hector Brown has to stay on the list of suspects.

Do not get too disheartened that you haven't been able to rule anybody out. Investigations include many red herrings and setbacks. It's part of the job. But those who persevere are those who triumph! I mean, that's not always true, but people who persevere have a much better chance of success than those who don't. So, with that in mind, it's time to head back to the scene of the crime to see if there is any evidence you missed.

At Captain Phillips's office, you spend some time searching and discover a major breakthrough. You find a business card on the floor, near to where Captain Phillips was attacked.

There are some partial fingerprints on it. With your keen eyes, you may be able to determine to whom they belong.

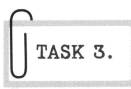

TASK 3.

Who left the fingerprints on the business card? Can you match the partial prints on the card to one of the suspects' full prints? Circle the suspect's name.

HECTOR BROWN

FATHER BARNABY

TYRONNE GRIGGS

PARTIAL PRINTS FROM CRIME SCENE

 HARTIGAN'S HINT: Look for noticeable patterns in the fingerprints.

Answer on page 203

This is simply staggering news! These fingerprints are proof that, of the three suspects caught on camera, Father Barnaby was the one who entered the office. He must be responsible for the theft of the Dumpleton Diamond and the attack on Captain Phillips! He was also at the church when Mavis set it on fire, so he must have been the one to blackmail her.

It's time to confront him with your findings. But when you go to St. Dingleby's church, it is eerily quiet. Not a soul is there. You sneak into a room in the back and find a crumpled piece of paper on the floor.

<u>Coordinates for the Cross</u>

A) He Leadeth Me ÷ How Can I Keep from Singing
Shine Jesus Shine - Once in Royal David's City

B) Away in a Manger - There's a Song in the Air
Give Me Oil in My Lamp - I Am a Pilgrim

C) He's Got the Whole World - Rock of Ages
I `ll Be a Sunbeam + ? = Eternal Father

D) He Leadeth Me ÷ Jerusalem
Colors of Day^2

HARTIGAN'S HINT: Colors of Day^2 means
Colors of Day × Colors of Day

There is an open hymn book on the table. This must be linked to the note you found.

EVIDENCE LOG 5.

Beside the note is a plan of St. Dingleby's church.
A coordinate grid has been placed over it.

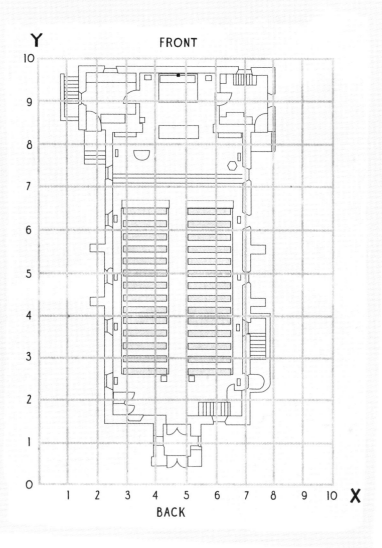

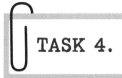

TASK 4.

First, you will need to find the missing numbers by using the hymns mentioned on the note and the page numbers they correspond to in the hymn book.

The first (x,y) coordinate is (2, ?)

The number 2 was determined by dividing "He Leadeth Me" (page 28) by "How Can I Keep from Singing" (page 14).

28÷14 = 2. Therefore, x = 2.

Then, once you have calculated your coordinates, turn the page to plot them on the grid.

Answer on page 204

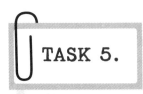
Find the missing digits and plot them on the coordinate grid. Remember the first number in parentheses refers to the x-axis, the second number refers to the y-axis.

Once you have identified all four coordinates, draw lines diagonally from points A to D and from B to C. Use a ruler or straight edge so that the lines are straight. (Detectives must be exacting!) The point where the lines of the cross intersect gives you a location.

Maybe this will reveal to you Father Barnaby's whereabouts, or perhaps it will lead you to the Dumpleton Diamond.

Time to get sleuthing! Your answer will move you on to **Case 6: Father, Where Art Thou?**

Answer on page 205

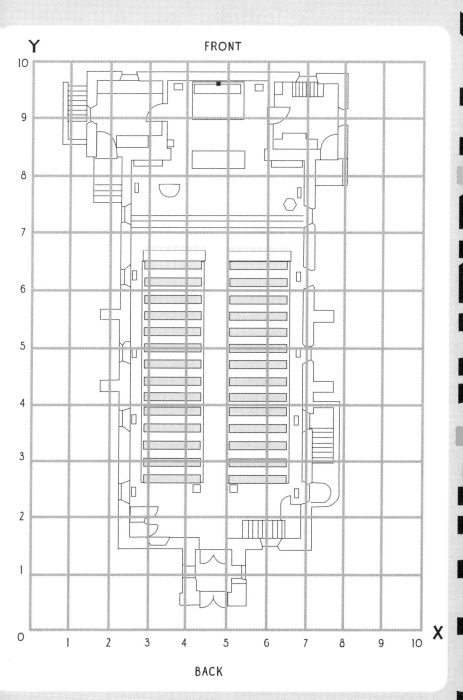

Y

FRONT

BACK

X

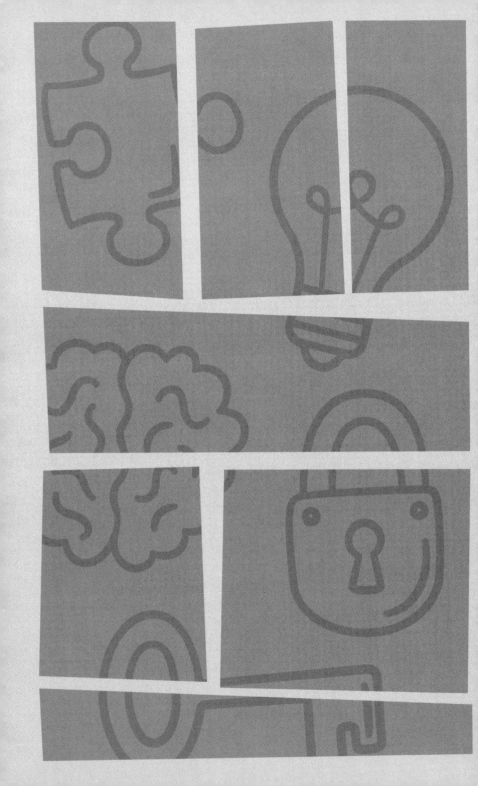

CASE 6:
FATHER, WHERE ART THOU?

Jolly good work, young detective! That took some determination to work out, but I know by now that you are the determined sort: You're not deterred by locked doors or missing keys, you've poured over historic records, and you've traversed across town to track down evidence and take witness statements.

And now, the intersection of the newest set of coordinates has led you to a row of pews. Your first instinct is to take a seat and a well-deserved rest, but this is no time for pause! We're closing in on the culprit now, so let's stay focused. Which row is of interest to you?

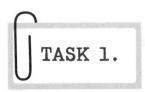

TASK 1.

Using the grid on page 123, count the pews from the front
of the church to determine the row letter. The front row is
row A.

Write your answer here:

When you get to the pew, the seats are labeled from left to right.
Which seat is of interest to you?

Write the letter here:

If you were to write this as A = 1, B = 2, etc.,

this would be row number

and seat number

Answer on page 206

When you reach the pew, you don't see anything unusual, but then you notice a small handle under seat 6. When you pull it, you leap back as the whole pew swings out and reveals a hatch in the floor below:

A trapdoor!

There's a combination lock on the top.

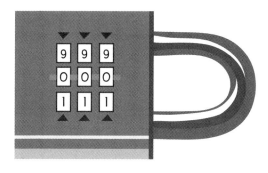

You have to find the correct three numbers in the correct order to open it! There are 1,000 possibilities—you simply don't have time to try them all with a felonious Father on the loose.

You look around for some clues and see a small piece of paper taped to the underside of the pew. Someone has left a reminder in case they forget the combination.

Combination total = F + F
The first number is 2
The numbers increase from left to right
All the numbers are even

Note taped to the underside
of the church pew

What's this? F and F again! That surely can't be a coincidence?

Notes:

  HARTIGAN'S HINT: To increase means to get bigger.

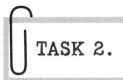

TASK 2.

Use the clues to figure out the three numbers in the correct order that will open the combination lock.

To crack this, you are going to first have to work out what $F + F$ equals. You have already done this with the row and seat numbers!

What is the combination total? F + F = _____

So the three numbers in the code must add up to that.
What is the code?

Write your answer here:

Answer on page 206

Wonderful—you're in! The trapdoor opens, and you descend down some steps and into a dark corridor underneath the church. Some might think this is spooky, but not you, my intrepid explorer! You find a light switch. The light cast from a single bulb is dim, but sufficient for you to make out six doors that lead from the corridor. Hanging from a hook on the wall is a wooden block. It is a peculiar shape, and you wonder what it is for.

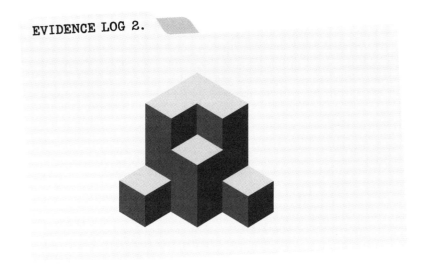

You notice that each of the doors has a shape cut into its large wooden handle. It appears that this strange wooden block is a key that will fit perfectly into one of the doors.

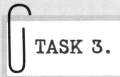

TASK 3.

Which door handle does the bottom of the wooden block fit? Circle the correct answer.

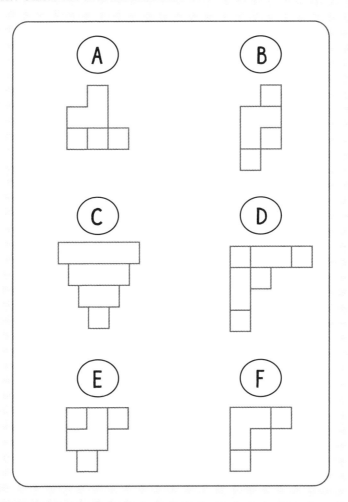

Answer on page 207

You open the door, and tentatively step inside. The room is empty, except for a table, and there is still no sign of Father Barnaby. You do notice two things on the table that might be of interest.

The first is a piece of paper with strange symbols on it. It seems to be a coded message. I believe this is a cipher known as the Pigpen Cipher. You need to figure out what it says as it may be important to the case.

Notes:

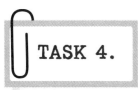

TASK 4.

Decipher the message and write the answer below.

EVIDENCE LOG 3.

A	B	C
D	E	F
G	H	I

```
    S
 T  ✕  U
    V
```

J·	K·	L·
M·	N·	O·
P	Q	R

```
    W
 X· ✕· Y
    Z
```

Cipher message:

∨ ⊓ □ ⊡

< Ė <

⊓ ⌐ ∧ □ Γ >

L ⊏ ⊐ □

⊓ ⊏ ⊐ □

⅂ ⌐ ⊡ ⅂ ⅂

What does the message say? _____

HARTIGAN'S HINT: Each symbol represents a letter on one of the four grids.

The second item on the table that is of interest to you is an ornate metal box. The top of it is patterned. On closer inspection, it seems to be some sort of dial lock.

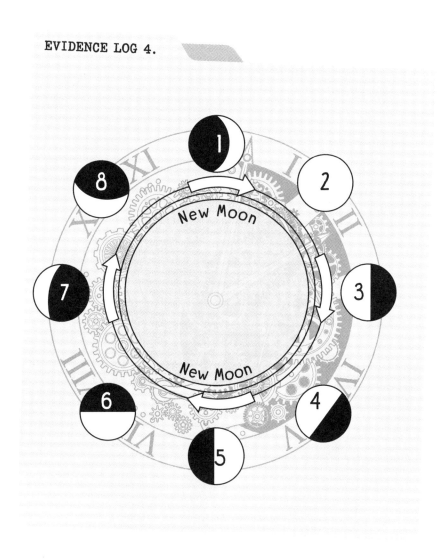

Something about it is familiar to you. You've seen these circles somewhere before. If you can't quite remember, do not worry, you have kept an excellent set of notes. Look back to Case 4 on page 103.

Yes! Of course, it is the same image as the one you found in Captain Phillips's father's diary! I bet you are glad you made a copy now.

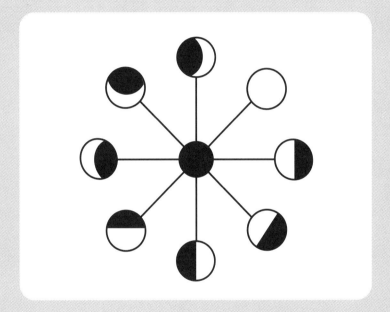

It shows the phases of the moon. But you found something about it peculiar.

Some of the phases aren't correct! Have a look at the actual phases of the moon on the next page.

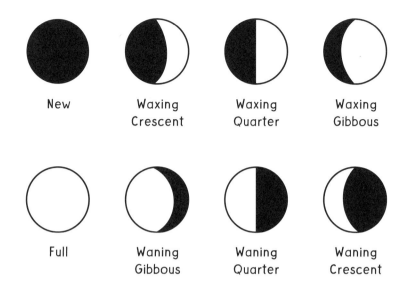

New	Waxing Crescent	Waxing Quarter	Waxing Gibbous
Full	Waning Gibbous	Waning Quarter	Waning Crescent

When you study the dial lock again, you realize that it doesn't spin, but the moons along the outer edge are able to slide into the middle—*the New Moon.*

You must slide the moons into the middle, but how are you supposed to know which ones to slide into which position?

You remember the note that you found in the diary:

> Everything starts with a New Moon.
> Crescents wax, then quarter.
> Then crescents wane and quarter.
> Always in that order.

It's a clue to unlocking the box! It tells you the *order* of the moons.

The New Moon is the largest circle in the center of the lock; you press it, and four round holes appear, labeled A–D.

You have to correctly match and "slide" each of four moons from the outer edge into its corresponding center hole.

Notice how the moons on the dial are in the same position as the ones you sketched from the diary. You need to work out which ones are true phases of the moon and which ones are incorrect. Do not select a false moon!

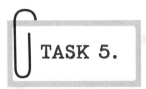

TASK 5.

Write the correct number in moons A–D.

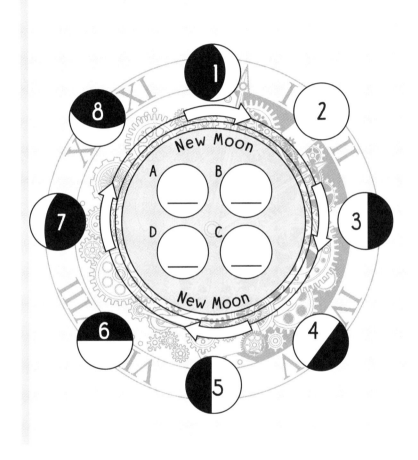

 HARTIGAN'S HINT: You need to start with a waxing crescent. Some
moons are there to trick you, so look out for ones that are rotated into an
incorrect position. You don't want to choose those!

Answer on page 209

138

WOWSERS!

It's a WHOPPER!

You have found the Dumpleton Diamond!

The lights suddenly go out. Someone pushes you. If it's Father Barnaby, pushing is certainly *not* something he would preach to do, but then, you suppose, neither is putting a bucket over somebody's head and stealing a diamond from them. And you can't be certain it is him. You call out his name, but there is no answer.

There's a rummaging noise. Then the slam of the door. You scramble in the dark for the light switch. You manage to turn it on and when you do, you see that the diamond is gone! Someone's made off with it again!

Hurry! It's on to **Case 7: The Chase for the Villain!**

Discoveries so far:

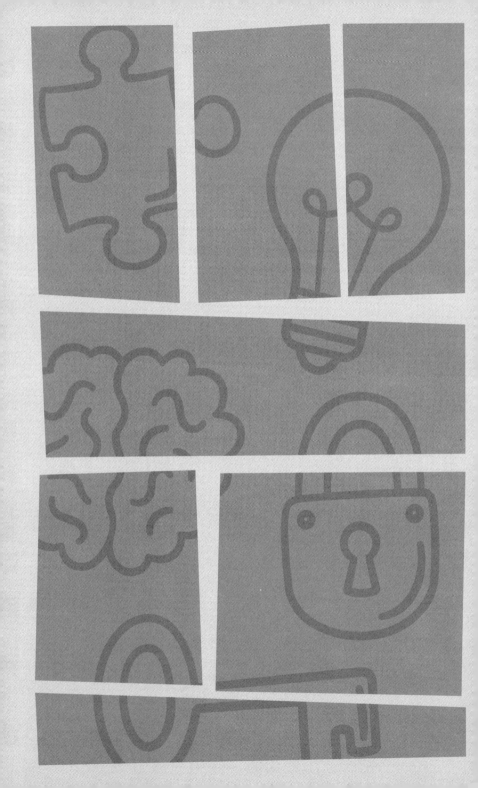

CASE 7:

THE CHASE
FOR THE VILLAIN

You rush to the door in hot pursuit of whomever stole the Dumpleton Diamond, but when you try the handle, it is locked. You try to force it open by charging at it with your shoulder. That does not go well for you, and you're glad that no one is around to witness you ricochet off the door and land on your backside.

You decide to use your intellect instead of brute force and look around the room for something to use in place of the block key.

You look back in your casebook to see what it looks like.

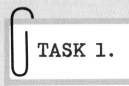

There are some wooden blocks on a shelf nearby. You could use these to make your own key!

Key you need to replicate

Circle the pieces you need:

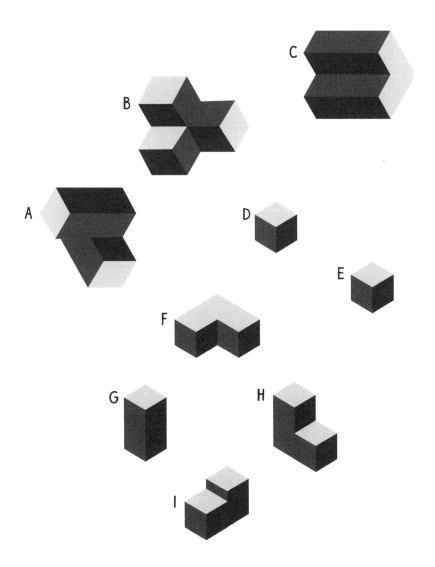

 HARTIGAN'S HINT: You need four pieces, including one large and two that match.

Answer on page 210

Hurrah! You're out! You race along the corridor and climb back out of the trapdoor into the church. You catch sight of someone charging out of the front and head after them.

As they jump into a taxi, something falls out of their pocket. They speed off and you bend down to pick up what they dropped. It's an envelope—a rather fancy one. There's no name on the front, and nothing inside, but when you look at the flap you notice a flower pattern and a message written in code.

EVIDENCE LOG 1.

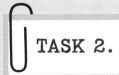

TASK 2.

You've seen this code before. It's the Pigpen Cipher from page 133. You need to work out what it says quickly! It might give you a clue as to where Father Barnaby is headed. If it *is* Father Barnaby.

The code says: _____

_____

_____

There's that last name again! It must have some bearing on your investigation. It's too much of a coincidence for it to keep popping up. There is also an address: The Lodge, Pucklebury. Perhaps it's the address of the sender. It definitely sounds familiar.

You call for a taxi to take you there, but the driver, Gordon, is new and only has a vague memory of how to get to The Lodge as he's only been there once before. He hands you a map so you can help him with the directions.

Answer on page 211

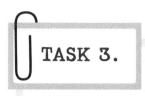

TASK 3.

From what Gordon can remember, use the map to determine where The Lodge is.

Place an ✗ on the map where you believe it is.

1. We'll come in on a road and there'll be a church on our right.

2. We'll take a sharp right turn and keep going until we get to a roundabout.

3. It's either the first or second turn off the roundabout.

4. But I remember a little way down the road there'll be a post office on our left. Or was it the right? There's definitely a post office.

5. Anyway, we'll continue on that road and cross over a river. There's another church. One with a steeple. Oh, that reminds me! When we first came into Pucklebury, the church on the right was one with a tower.

6. Then there's a bit of broken wall, which is apparently of historical significance, on the right. People drive miles to see it. Can't see the fuss myself.

7. Right after the wall, it's either a right-hand turn or a left-hand turn. One of them'll be correct because, there you go! Bob's your uncle, Fanny's your aunt—The Lodge is opposite an elementary school and next to a pond. How's that for memory!

 HARTIGAN'S HINT: Read through all of the directions before you draw your route.

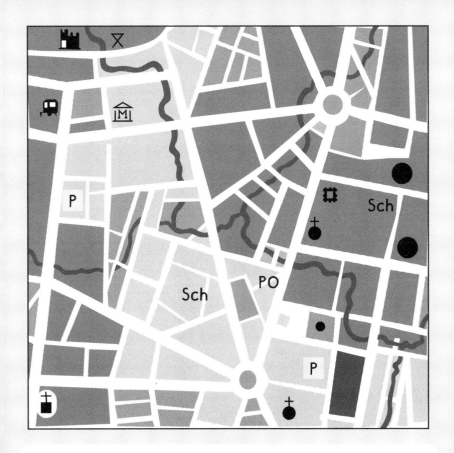

KEY:

PO	Post Office	P	Parking
	Castle		Campsite
Sch	School	M̂	Museum
♦	Church (steeple)	⬚	Heritage Site
▪	Church (tower)	✕	Picnic Area
●	Pond		

You thank Gordon for taking you to The Lodge. Before you enter, you make a phone call to the police station to share your findings. You tell them you believe Father Barnaby has the Dumpleton Diamond, has been blackmailing Mavis Bold, and is responsible for the attack on Captain Phillips. You hope you're right.

Notes:

There are some security gates outside The Lodge. When you try them, they are locked. You don't think anyone is going to let you through if you buzz the intercom, so you are going to have to find a way to open them yourself. There is a box at one side of the gates. You open it to find a tangle of wires: the electronics that open and shut the gates.

You need to work out which wires open the sliding left and right gates. Two correct numbers, from 1–8, must be pressed at the same time to initiate the opening mechanism.

HARTIGAN'S HINT: Look at the sliding gates. In which direction does each gate need to move to open? Look at the arrows.

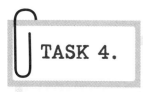

TASK 4.

The gates are not the kind that swing open; these gates slide back and forth. Follow the electrical wires from the correct direction buttons to determine which numbered buttons open the left and right gates.

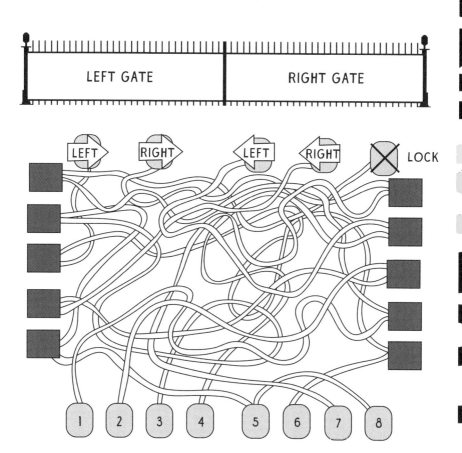

Answer on page 213

153

Hooray! The gates open and you walk up the driveway to The Lodge. The door opens before you have a chance to knock. It is Father Barnaby, and he's smiling.

"I've been expecting you. Please, come inside."

You hesitate. Could this be a trap? Knowing that the police are on their way, you enter the house and follow Father Barnaby to a very nice living room. There are two older people there—one sitting in an armchair, the other on a plush sofa.

"May I introduce my parents," Father Barnaby says. "Petunia and Cyril Forsyth."

Father Barnaby's last name is Forsyth! Just like the names on the gravestone. It all makes sense now. His parents are the M AND D—Mom and Dad—from the Pigpen Cipher note on page 133!

He gestures to a sofa, and you sit. He remains standing.

Cyril Forsyth crosses his legs and leans back in his chair. "So, you're the kid who's been snooping into matters that don't concern you."

"I'm afraid if you're after the Dumpleton Diamond, you've wasted your time," Petunia says.

Father Barnaby begins pacing the room. "The Dumpleton Diamond belongs to the Forsyth family. Perhaps the methods by which it came into our possession were a little underhanded, but it was won by Bandit the ferret, fair and square-ish. I know Captain Phillips believes it is his family heirloom, but he is wrong! We have been trying to locate it for years!"

Cyril clears his throat. "Our ancestor, Marmaduke Forsyth, hid the Dumpleton Diamond to keep it safe. He created the map so future generations would know where to find it." He casts an accusatory look at Petunia. "The map was lost years ago after a particularly zealous spring clean and somehow ended up in Harold Phillips's possession."

Petunia bristles. "You should have kept it somewhere safe. How was I to know you'd hidden it inside *Lawn Bowling: A Maintenance Guide*?"

"Because I told you! And I didn't think anyone would ever read such a tiresome tome!" Cyril argues.

You ask how he knew about the map hidden behind *The Flying Goat.*

"I discovered that horrendous painting was a clue to the diamond's whereabouts at a dinner party in London where I met an artist named Basil van Goof. I mentioned I was from Little Dumpleton, and he told me he had once been commissioned to paint something to hide a map of my village."

You flash the card you found in Captain Phillips's office.

"Ah, yes," Father Barnaby says. "He gave me his card. I think my interest led him to believe that I might wish to purchase one of his dreadful paintings. But there was only one I wanted, *The Flying Goat*, and I had to get it without Phillips knowing. I couldn't risk him discovering I was on the verge of solving the mystery of where the Dumpleton Diamond was hidden."

Is that why he blackmailed Mavis?

"Anyway . . ." Father Barnaby leans against the fireplace, "it turned out Captain Phillips was further along in his own investigation than I had anticipated. He made it to the monument just before I did. I couldn't believe it! I had to do something, so when I saw he was heading to his office, I retrieved the key from his house, then followed him there and took the diamond for myself."

Cyril leans forward and chuckles. "The only problem Barnaby had—in fact, the only problem generations of Forsyths have had—was how to get the diamond out of that blasted box! I believe we have *you* to thank for solving that conundrum!"

There's a knock at the door. Petunia rises to her feet. "I suppose that will be the police. What a shame they've wasted a trip out here."

Two police officers come into the sitting room. Petunia offers them tea and they decline. When they say they are here about the theft of the Dumpleton Diamond and an attack on the Captain, the Forsyths play innocent and say they know nothing about the diamond and the attack.

When you chime in to tell the police you have proof that Father Barnaby is a crook, they listen, but one of them cuts you off and says, "It sounds like you've had a very exciting time." Then he winks at Father Barnaby and says, "The imagination of the young, am I right?"

You protest and take out your casebook, but before you can even begin to explain about Dave the teacup terrier, or ferret maze runners, or *The Flying Goat*, the police officer says, "I'm afraid if there's no diamond, there is no evidence, and therefore no crime."

"There is no Dumpleton Diamond. Feel free to search the house if you don't believe me," Cyril says, a sly smile on his lips.

He's bluffing! The diamond is here! And Father Barnaby couldn't have had long to hide it. Your detective instincts kick in. He's got to be. The diamond is in the very room you are standing in. You just know it! There must be a clue somewhere.

TASK 5.

What do your detective instincts tell you? Where would you look for the Dumpleton Diamond?

 HARTIGAN'S HINT: F and F

Answer on page 214

The painting of Albert and Ruth Forsyth—F and F! Their names have come up frequently throughout your investigation. It is the most likely hiding place.

You look more closely at the picture and see there is a hinge on one side. You open it up and discover a safe behind it.

When you ask the police officers to tell the Forsyths to open the safe, they tell you they can't without a search warrant.

Cyril says, "Oh, we would, but the combination was lost when dear Albert and Ruth passed—the correct numbers rest with them."

"You're more than welcome to try," Petunia says. She gives you a condescending look. She thinks you can't! But she shouldn't underestimate you. It's time for your final case, **Case 8: Dial for Detective**.

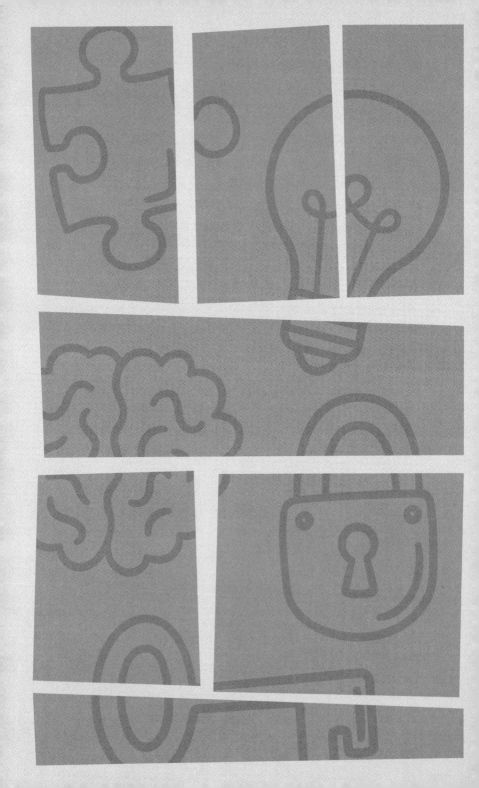

CASE 8:
DIAL FOR DETECTIVE

The police have given you five minutes to try to open the safe. They do not want to inconvenience the Forsyths any longer.

FINAL TASK

The dial lock requires you to turn the dial to the starting position by the arrow eight times. This means you need to know eight numbers. They could be anything from 0–99. The possibilities are endless. You cannot guess. But you don't need to. You already know what the numbers are.

Remember, these are the Forsyths you are dealing with. And Cyril accidentally gave you a clue: *The correct numbers rest with them.* Where have you found a code with eight numbers before? Look back through your case notes and when you have found the combination, write it in the boxes.

You put in your numbers, the safe springs open, and there, sitting inside, is the Dumpleton Diamond.

 HARTIGAN'S HINT: Cemetery on p. 80

Answer on page 214

You hand your case notes over to the police officers and tell them that everything they need to charge Father Barnaby is inside. The police officer flicks through the pages, shakes his head, and says, "Poor Furblast never stood a chance."

Father Barnaby is led away in handcuffs to face the full force of the law. And you, young detective, will have earned your first detective badge once you hand over the diamond. What, you didn't think you'd get to keep it, did you?

I'm sure you will agree that seeing justice served is the greatest reward. Bravo! You, as I suspected, have turned out to be a very fine detective. A very fine detective indeed! In fact, I might have to see about sending you out on another case.

THE
DUMPLETON DAILY

BARNABY CAUGHT RED-HANDED!

In news that has shaken the whole of Rompingshire, Little Dumpleton's very own Father Barnaby Forsyth has been charged with blackmail and battery related to the theft of the Dumpleton Diamond!

It is believed that a new recruit from the world-renowned Hartigan Browne Detective Agency was responsible for exposing Father Barnaby's criminal antics.

The once well-respected Forsyth family, currently residing in Pucklebury, appears to have had underhanded dealings with the Dumpleton Diamond for generations.

In 1933, the Forsyths first got their hands on the diamond after Marmaduke Forsyth cheated in a game of ferret maze running against then-owner Ernest Phillips.

While the search starts for a new vicar, the community remains rocked by these recent revelations.

Peter Knox said, "I knew that Father Barnaby was a wrong'un ever since he placed my squash in second at this year's Largest Vegetable Competition."

Mavis Bold, who was blackmailed by Father Barnaby over her involvement in the church fire years ago, said, "I'm glad everything's out in the open. I haven't been able to listen to Taylor Swift for guilt over that fire, but I think I might finally be able to enjoy her music again."

Father Barnaby, however, has found no such peace, and it is believed he will plead not guilty to the charges brought against him.

With such strong evidence against him, it would be surprising if he were acquitted. The case made by Hartigan Browne's new recruit has been described as airtight.

All the Father can do now is pray.

WORD LINKERS!

What word can be placed on the end of the first word and the start of the second to create two new words or phrases?

BOWLING	_____	ROOM
HAIR	_____	STROKE
CUP	_____	WALK

LET THE GOOD TIMES BOWL!

After a two-year break following the fight that hospitalized two villagers and left a mobility vehicle submerged in the local pond, Little Dumpleton's lawn bowling team, Bowl Movements, is back and looking for new members.

If you're keen to try your arm, pop along to the green any Thursday afternoon. We prefer you to wear white, and anyone sporting Lycra will be asked to leave the league immediately.

And on that note, please remember that while we encourage competitive play, the umpire's decision is final. Anyone arguing with the umpire will also be removed.

DRAWING
DUMP GOOF?

Little Dumpleton is in an uproar following the commission of Basil van Goof to paint this year's village calendar. Ivanna Craft, owner of Little Dumpleton's art gallery, The Drawing Dump, chose van Goof for his interesting and unique style and believes that this year's calendar will move the village into the twenty-first century.

Local man Hector Brown describes van Goof's style as an "abomination" and considers it a scandal that his suggestion of *Portraits of Cattle Throughout the Seasons* was rejected.

If you would like to join the protest outside The Drawing Dump, it will start this Tuesday from 11:30 a.m. It is advised to bring a hot thermos and to bundle up as it can get a bit blustery outside the gallery.

IS FINKLEBOTTOM STUFFED?

The inquest continues into the allegations that Gavin Finklebottom stuffed his squash with flour to win first prize at the Largest Vegetable Competition. Gavin refutes this, but Dianne Collins has recently confirmed that the week before the competition, she did give him several bags of out-of-date self-rising flour that she had stored out back in her bakery.

Answer on page 215

167

FURBLAST THE FELON

Much to Captain Phillips's dismay, doubt has been cast as to whether he is the rightful owner of the Dumpleton Diamond following the discovery of an old newspaper article dating back to 1929.

The word *ferret* is derived from the Latin *furittus*, meaning little thief, and it would appear to be with good reason. Information has surfaced that strongly suggests Furblast was used to steal the Dumpleton Diamond from Lady Esmerelda Collins, a distant relative of Dianne Collins.

Dianne has confirmed she will be pursuing ownership of the diamond. "Honestly, I didn't think this year could get any better after I won the Knobbliest Knees Competition for a third time! But if it is true that Furblast stole the diamond when Esmerelda was cooling off in the duck pond, it is only right that it should be returned to the Collins family."

WHO WON THIS WEEK'S VILLAGE BINGO?

The winner arrived on time and was wearing a scarf. Who got lucky this week?

	Early	Late	On Time	Hat	Glasses	Scarf
Dianne						
Mavis						
Morris						
Hat						
Glasses						
Scarf						

1. The person wearing glasses was not on time.

2. Morris doesn't wear glasses and is never early.

3. The person who was late isn't wearing glasses.

4. Dianne didn't arrive early, and she wasn't wearing a hat because she'd just had her hair done.

5. The person who arrived on time wasn't wearing a hat.

Answer on page 215

DUMPLETON'S DAILY CROSSWORD

ACROSS

[3] Day of the protest against Basil van Goof

[6] Where Lady Esmerelda was when Furblast stole the diamond

[7] Substance Gavin Finklebottom allegedly used to stuff his squash

[8] What county would you find Little Dumpleton in?

[9] Last name of the singer whom Mavis can once again listen to

DOWN

[1] First name of Furblast's owner

[2] Whose portraits did Hector Brown suggest should feature in the village calendar?

[4] Word Hector Brown uses to describe Basil van Goof's painting style

[5] First name of the ferret maze cheat

[7] Latin for "little thief"

MODELS WANTED FOR TYRONNE'S TRIMS

Tyronne Griggs is seeking models for experimental hairstyling.

Tyronne is excited to branch out into the world of competitive hairdressing and he needs models to practice on to achieve his dream. If you want a style upgrade for free and fancy making a statement, pop along to the salon and sign up.

NOTE: Hairstyling may include the use of glue and staple guns, low-grade cement, and goose fat. More intricate designs may involve metalwork with the possibility of some welding, so please be prepared to withstand high temperatures.

Answer on page 215

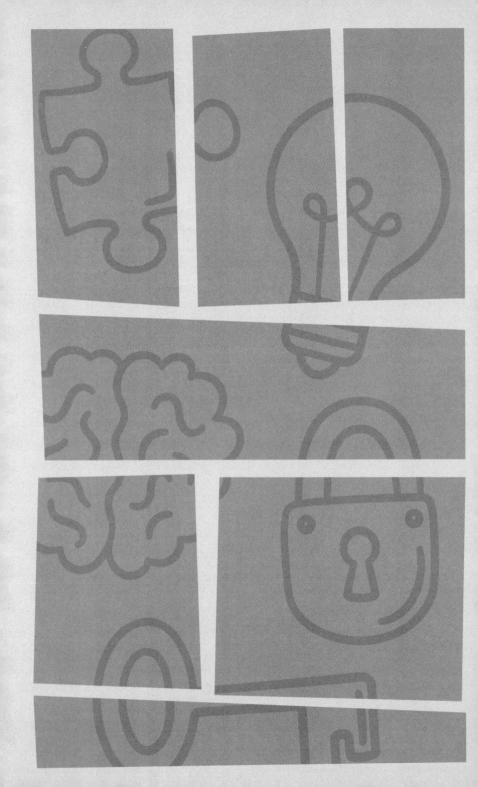

ANSWERS

ANSWERS:
AGENT SELECTION

TASK 1.
From page 2

You should have circled *no*. If you solved the code and circled *yes*, frankly, I have no words.

A R E   Y O U   A   N I T W I T ?

C I R C L E   A N S W E R :

Y E S / NO

TASK 2.

From page 4

Gear A must be turned counterclockwise.

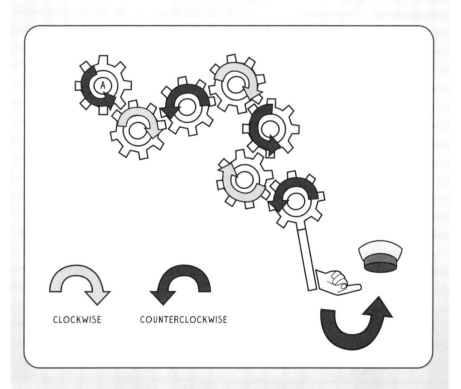

CLOCKWISE   COUNTERCLOCKWISE

TASK 3.

From page 6

The coordinates were G,O so you need to find the **G** on the
x-axis and then the **O** on the y-axis. You are heading to Little
Dumpleton.

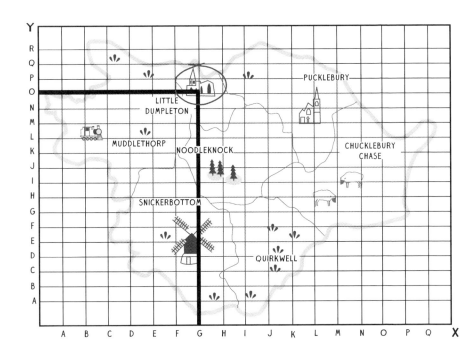

TASK 4.
From page 10

The answer is pattern B.

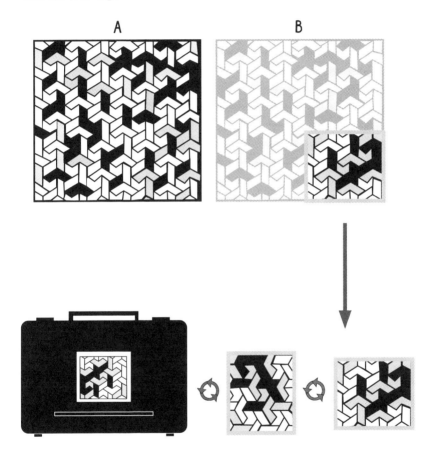

The section has been rotated 180 degrees.

ANSWERS:
CASE 1: PUP, PUP, AND AWAY!

TASK 1.
From page 23

9:00 A.M.-10:00 A.M.	Quilting Demonstration
11:30 A.M.-12:30 P.M.	Best Cake Competition
2:00 P.M.-3:00 P.M.	Largest Vegetable Competition
3:30 P.M.-4:00 P.M.	Knobbliest Knees Competition

TASK 2.

From page 24

NAME	At festival at the time of the Veg Comp.	In the tent during Veg Comp.
MAVIS BOLD	✔	✘
TYRONNE GRIGGS	✔	✔
FRED LITTLE	✔	✘
DIANNE COLLINS	✔	✔
FATHER BARNABY	✔	✔
MORRIS NORRIS	✔	✘

NAME	At festival at the time of the Veg Comp.	In the tent during Veg Comp.
HECTOR BROWN	✔	✘
CAPTAIN PHILLIPS	✘	✘
SALLY PHILLIPS	✘	✘
GAVIN FINKLEBOTTOM	✔	✔
PETER KNOX	✔	✔
BARBARA NOVAK	✘	✘

TASK 3.
From page 26

1	MAVIS BOLD
2	FRED LITTLE
3	MORRIS NORRIS
4	HECTOR BROWN

TASK 4.
From page 27

A hot dog was used to subdue Dave.

Name	In possession of hot dog?
MAVIS BOLD	✔
FRED LITTLE	✔
MORRIS NORRIS	✘
HECTOR BROWN	✔

Morris Norris was the only one who did not have the time to visit the hot dog stand, so you can eliminate him from your inquiries.

TASK 6.
From page 30

HANDSAW	CAKE KNIFE	KITCHEN KNIFE	PINKING SHEARS	ANGLED SHEARS	GARDENING CLIPPERS
HECTOR B	FATHER B MAVIS B FRED L DIANNE C	FRED L HECTOR B	MAVIS B DIANNE C BARBARA N	MORRIS N	GAVIN F

TASK 7.
From page 32

Accusation:

The perpetrator was **Mavis Bold**!

T	H	I	S	C	H	U	R	C	H
82	81	80	79	78	77	76	75	74	73
O	F	S	T	D	I	N	G	L	E
72	71	70	69	68	67	66	65	64	63
B	Y	S	W	A	S	E	R	E	C
62	61	60	59	58	57	56	55	54	53
T	E	D	I	N	T	H	E	Y	E
52	51	50	49	48	47	46	45	44	43
A	R	E	I	G	H	T	E	E	N
42	41	40	39	38	37	36	35	34	33
S	I	X	T	Y	F	I	V	E	F
32	31	30	29	28	27	26	25	24	23
O	R	T	H	E	P	A	R	I	S
22	21	20	19	18	17	16	15	14	13
H	O	F	D	U	M	P	L	E	T
12	11	10	9	8	7	6	5	4	3
O	N								
2	1								

Each letter from the note has been inserted into the grid. The numbers 82–1 have been inserted in descending order below the letters. To work out the coded message, you need to find the letter that matches each number. The first three numbers in the coded message have been circled in the grid to show you.

This Church of St. Dingleby's was erected in the year eighteen sixty-five for the Parish of Dumpleton.

Y O U   S T A R T E D
(61, 72, 76)   (79, 82, 58, 75, 69, 63, 68)

T H E   F I R E.
(52, 77, 56) (71, 80, 55, 54).

G E T   T H E
(65, 51, 47) (36, 73, 45)

F L Y I N G   G O A T
(27, 64, 44, 67, 66, 38) (65, 22, 42, 29)

F O R   M Y   S I L E N C E.
(10, 11, 41) (7, 28) (70, 49, 5, 43, 48, 78, 40).

ANSWERS:
CASE 2: MISBEHAVING MAVIS

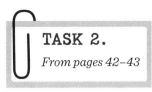

TASK 2.
From pages 42–43

```
E  C  O  N  T  R  A  C  T  N  V  C
V  Z  N  K  E  F  U  O  W  R  E  J
L  O  E  F  S  M  O  N  E  Y  O  M
O  Y  X  E  E  S  F  H  W  P  L
S  R  B  M  V  A  S  E  L  E  R  Y
O  O  S  P  M  L  T  S  F  E  O  F
S  Q  S  R  E  I  A  S  S  Z  P  G
Z  U  O  W  E  B  T  I  A  B  E  N
L  I  E  N  Z  I  U  O  I  P  R  S
S  J  P  W  A  T  E  N  A  O  T  F
O  O  Z  O  A  P  O  L  O  G  Y  W
T  U  P  E  W  Z  O  E  E  P  K  E
```

Mavis wanted a **painting** from Ivanna.

TASK 3.

From page 45

In these 6 × 6 sudoku puzzles, each 3 × 2 block, each row, and each column must contain the numbers 1–6 exactly once.

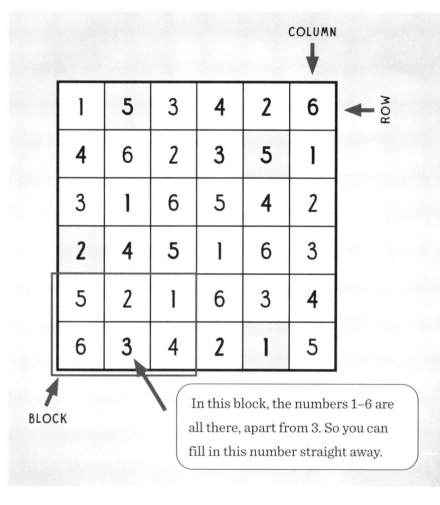

COLUMN

ROW

1	5	3	4	2	6
4	6	2	3	5	1
3	1	6	5	4	2
2	4	5	1	6	3
5	2	1	6	3	4
6	3	4	2	1	5

BLOCK

In this block, the numbers 1–6 are all there, apart from 3. So you can fill in this number straight away.

The four-digit passcode is **5521**.

TASK 4.

From page 46

Log Number	Article Description
FA001	Fascinating Find! A maze used for ferret racing has been unearthed in the fields at the back of Captain Phillips's house . . .
FA002	Father Barnaby Cries Holy Smoke! St. Dingleby's church, the heart of Little Dumpleton, has suffered a terrible fire . . .
FE001	Fenced In! Firefighters called out after Fred Little gets head stuck in the railings around the village pond. Villagers are being advised to proceed with caution when feeding the ducks.
FI001	Fight breaks out during hotly contested lawn bowling tournament, leaving two members of the Women's Association concussed and one mobility vehicle submerged in the village pond . . .
FI002	Finger Bun Inferno at Brilliant Buns . . .
FI003	Finklebottom blames hungry badgers for the loss of his turnip crop . . .
FL001	Flaming Fiasco: A Hair-Raising Episode at Tyronne's Trims!
FR002	Fred Little's frightful discovery as he realized he has been posting his letter in the dog waste bin for two years . . .

TASK 5.

From page 50

C = "Holy Smoke," of course! It would appear that Mavis may have more involvement in the fire at the church than the news story implies.

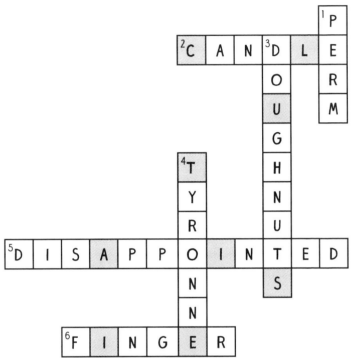

The letters in the gray squares:

C L U T A I S I E

Become . . .

I T I S A C L U E.

ANSWERS:
CASE 3: THE MYSTERY
OF THE FLYING GOAT

TASK 1.
From page 61

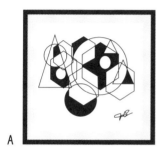

A

B

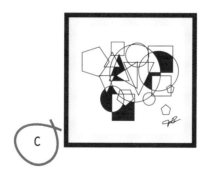

C

The painting you need to look at is **C** because it is the only one with triangles, squares, pentagons, and circles, as shown on the door handle.

TASK 2.

From page 63

The code is **5445**.

TASK 3.
From page 66

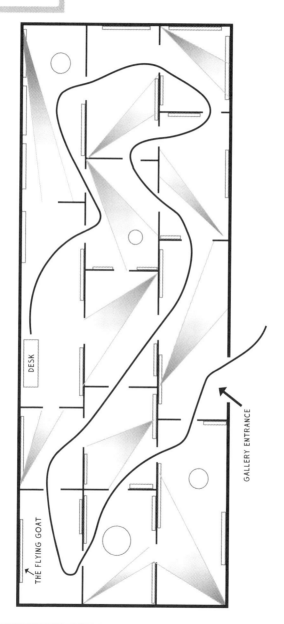

TASK 4.

From page 69

Ivanna told you that Dave the dog is her first pet. You had to take an educated guess at her favorite subject, but with her owning an art gallery, art seemed like the best option.

RESET USER PASSWORD

Answer the following questions:

Question 1: What is the name of your first pet?

Answer: D A V E

Question 2: What was your favorite subject in school?

Answer: A R T

The clue in this puzzle is the letters that spell out GOAT twice. Each letter in GOAT is attached to another letter; when those letters are rearranged, they make two new words.

The first GOAT spells out TURN
And the second GOAT spells out OVER
So turn over the painting!

TASK 6.

From page 76

From the start—your final destination is **St. Dingleby's Church**.

- **N** is the **fifth** letter in **A** (St. Di**n**gleby's Church). Go **AT** this number of paces.

- You should be at a village site (Monument). The second **N** is the **seventh** letter in **J** (Monume**n**t). Go **T** this number of paces.

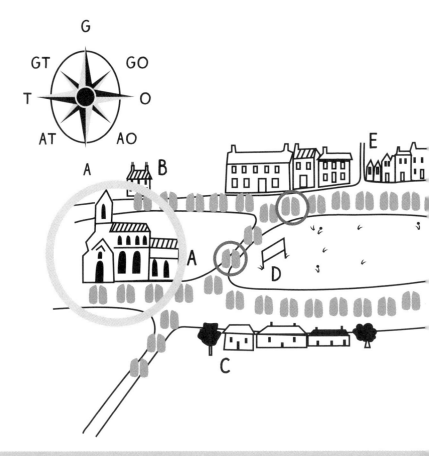

- From here, if you look **GO** ↗ you should see an important milk producer for the village (Dumplet**O**n Farm). **O** in this landmark is the **eighth** letter. Go **T** ← this number of paces.
- **N** is the **third** letter in K (Po**n**d). Go **AT** ↙ this number of paces.
- You should find yourself between two landmarks (St. Dingleby's Church and Village Green). The landmark to your **T** ← is your final destination.

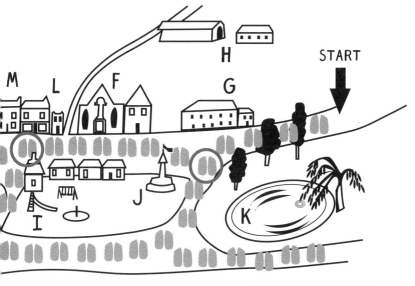

LITTLE DUMPLETON

TASK 7.
From page 78

It's **C**! Well done, you saw that the letters which start each line of the poem are **AFRF**—Albert Forsyth and Ruth Forsyth.

A

IN MEMORY
OF
ALICE COLLINS

1794 – 1881

WHO DISCOVERED
SHE COULD
NOT SWIM

MAY SHE
REST IN PEACE

FOREVER LOVED

B

IN MEMORY
OF
HORACE BROWN

WHO LOVED
HIS COWS.
MAY YOUR
HEAVENLY
FARM
PROSPER

1801 – 1869

C

HERE LIES
ALBERT FORSYTH
AND HIS WIFE
RUTH FORSYTH

7 – 72 – 66 – 76 – 7 – 63 – 48 – 69

TASK 8.

From page 80

To solve this one, you needed to use the grid you completed on page 39.

T	H	I	S	C	H	U	R	C	H
82	81	80	79	78	77	76	75	74	73
O	F	S	T	D	I	N	G	L	E
72	71	70	69	68	67	66	65	64	63
B	Y	S	W	A	S	E	R	E	C
62	61	60	59	58	57	56	55	54	53
T	E	D	I	N	T	H	E	Y	E
52	51	50	49	48	47	46	45	44	43
A	R	E	I	G	H	T	E	E	N
42	41	40	39	38	37	36	35	34	33
S	I	X	T	Y	F	I	V	E	F
32	31	30	29	28	27	26	25	24	23
O	R	T	H	E	P	A	R	I	S
22	21	20	19	18	17	16	15	14	13
H	O	F	D	U	M	P	L	E	T
12	11	10	9	8	7	6	5	4	3
O	N								
2	1								

M O N U M E N T

7 – 72 – 66 – 76 – 7 – 63 – 48 – 69

Hector is wearing jeans and green shoes.

Father Barnaby is wearing a suit and black shoes.

Captain Phillips is wearing chinos and brown shoes.

		Shoe color			Pants worn		
		BROWN	GREEN	BLACK	JEANS	CHINOS	SUIT
Suspects	HECTOR	✘	✔	✘	✔	✘	✘
	BARNABY	✘	✘	✔	✘	✘	✔
	CAPTAIN P.	✔	✘	✘	✘	✔	✘
Pants worn	JEANS	✘	✔	✘			
	CHINOS	✔	✘	✘			
	SUIT	✘	✘	✔			

TASK 10.

From page 84

Gavin saw **Captain Phillips**, so you are heading to

Dumpleton Manor.

ANSWERS:
CASE 4: FURBLAST

TASK 1.
From page 90

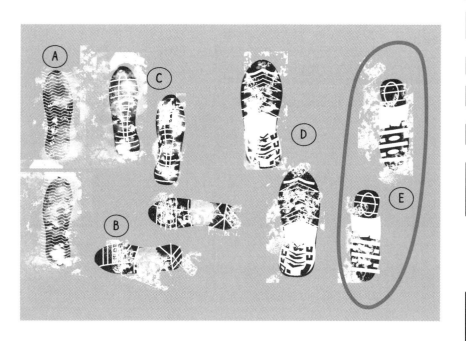

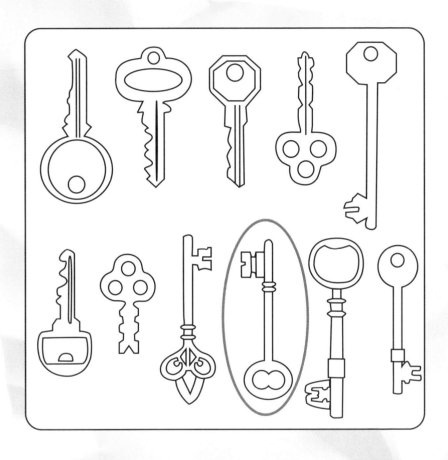

No. It was not possible for Furblast to win the race.

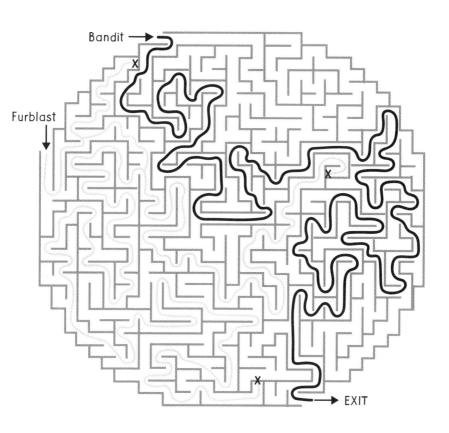

TASK 4.
From page 102

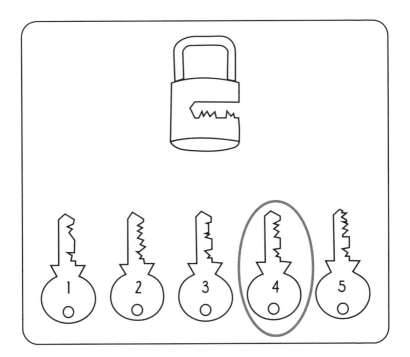

TASK 5.
From page 105

The code is **7942**.

ANSWERS:
CASE 5: PARTIALLY THERE

From page 109

No—Father Barnaby, Hector Brown, and Tyronne Griggs were all at the art gallery.

TASK 1.
From page 111

The letter **s** was used in each writing sample. It is the same type of **s** in two. You are left with **Father Barnaby** and **Hector Brown**.

Writing on envelope: *Mavis Bold*

HANDWRITING SAMPLES

Father Barnaby: *Psalm 23*

Hector Brown: *$1.29/lb. spuds*

Tyronne Griggs: *Short back n sides* $15.00

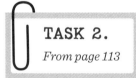

TASK 2.
From page 113

No, the footprint does not match. But it is a match for Captain Phillips's boots. They must wear the same type. This means you can't rule out Hector since you cannot be certain whether it was Captain Phillips's or Hector's footprints outside the back door.

TASK 3.
From page 115

HECTOR BROWN

FATHER BARNABY

TYRONNE GRIGGS

PARTIAL PRINTS FROM CRIME SCENE

From pages 117, 118, 119, and 121

Coordinates for the cross.

Point	Clue	Equation	Answer	Coordinate (x,y)
A	He Leadeth Me ÷ How Can I Keep from Singing	28 ÷ 14	2	(2,9)
	Shine Jesus Shine - Once in Royal David's City	78 - 69	9	
B	Away in a Manger - There's a Song in the Air	83 - 80	3	(3,2)
	Give Me Oil in My Lamp - I Am A Pilgrim	39 - 37	2	
C	He's Got the Whole World - Rock of Ages	59 - 52	7	(7,6)
	I'll Be a Sunbeam + ? = Eternal Father	64 + ? = 70	6	
D	He Leadeth Me ÷ Jerusalem	28 ÷ 4	7	(7,4)
	Colors of Day^2	22 or (2 × 2)	4	

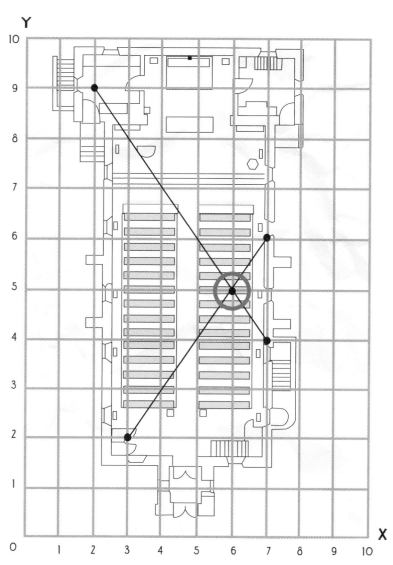

The location has the coordinates (6, 5).

ANSWERS:
CASE 6: FATHER, WHERE ART THOU?

TASK 1.
From page 126

Row: F, Seat: F

Or, Row: 6, Seat: 6.

TASK 2.
From page 129

F + F = 6 + 6 = 12. The numbers in the passcode must add up to 12.

Because the numbers increase left to right, the second number must be larger than 2.

237	NOT EVEN; NOT INCREASING	✘
246	EVEN AND INCREASING	✔
255	NOT EVEN; NOT INCREASING	✘
264	EVEN, BUT NOT INCREASING	✘
273	NOT EVEN; NOT INCREASING	✘
282	EVEN, BUT NOT INCREASING	✘
291	NOT EVEN; NOT INCREASING	✘

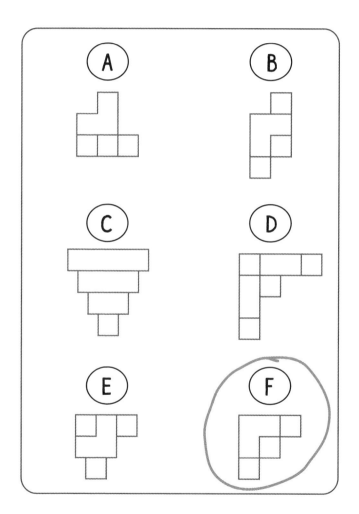

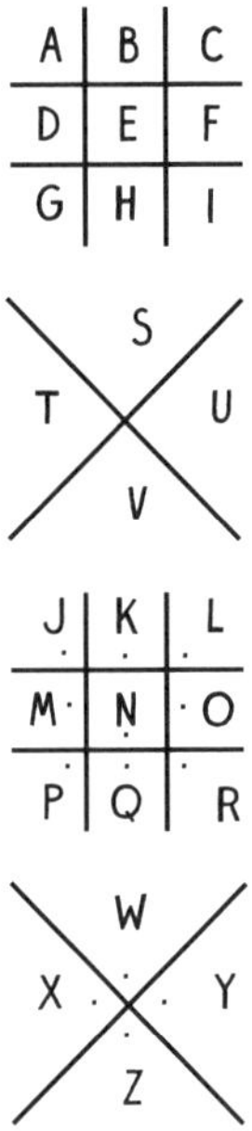

A	B	C
D	E	F
G	H	I

S
T · U
V

J	K	L
M	N	O
P	Q	R

W
X · · Y
Z

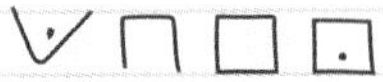

∨ ⊓ □ ⊡

W H E N

⟨ Ɛ ⟨

Y O U

⊓ ⅃ ∧ □ ⌐ ⟩

H A V E   I T

� ⊏⊡⊐ □

C O M E

⊓ ⊡ ⊐ □

H O M E

⅃ ⅃ ⊡ ⅃ ⅃

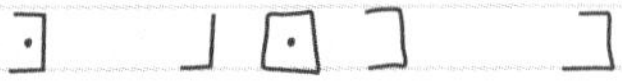

M   A N D   D

TASK 5.

From page 138

The inner circle represents a new moon, A is moon 1 (a waxing crescent), B is moon 5 (a waxing quarter), C is moon 7 (a waning crescent), and D is moon 3 (a waning quarter).

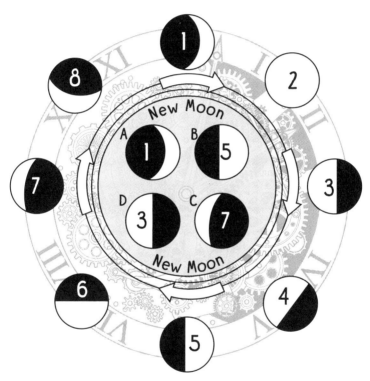

The poem tells you which four of the moon phases you need. *Everything starts with a New Moon* (the center). *Crescents wax* (waxing crescent), then *quarter* (waxing quarter). Then *crescents wane* (waning crescent) and *quarter* (waning quarter). *Always in that order.*

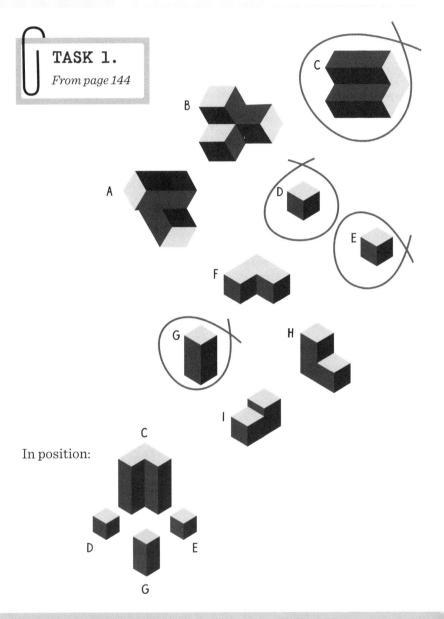

TASK 1.
From page 144

In position:

TASK 2.

From page 147

It is a return address! This must be the address of the sender.

FORSYTH

THE LODGE, PUCKLEBURY

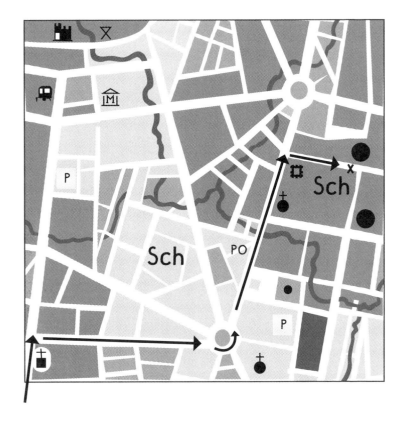

The correct numbers are 4 and 7.

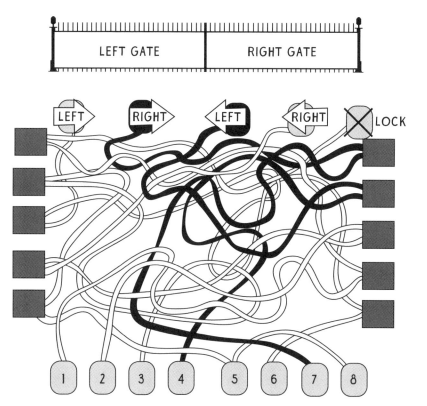

The gates need to open **outward**. The trick here is not to be confused by the arrows in the electrical box. They are organized according to the direction the gates move.

You need to take care to look at the arrow that opens the *left gate* in the correct direction and the arrow that opens the *right gate* in the correct direction.

TASK 5.
From page 159

The safe containing the diamond is hidden behind the painting of Albert and Ruth Forsyth.

ANSWERS:
CASE 8: DIAL FOR DETECTIVE

FINAL TASK
From page 164

The code is the numbers found on the gravestone of Albert and Ruth Forsyth.

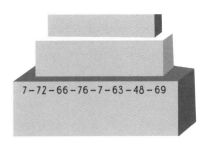

7 – 72 – 66 – 76 – 7 – 63 – 48 – 69

ANSWERS: DUMPLETON DAILY

From pages 167, 168, and 169

Word Linkers!

BOWLING	**BALL**	ROOM
HAIR	**BRUSH**	STROKE
CUP	**CAKE**	WALK

Who won this week's village bingo?

Dianne won. She arrived on time and was wearing a scarf.

	Early	Late	On Time	Hat	Glasses	Scarf
Dianne	X	X	✔	X	X	✔
Mavis	✔	X	X	X	✔	X
Morris	X	✔	X	✔	X	X
Hat	X	✔	X			
Glasses	✔	X	X			
Scarf	X	X	✔			

Dumpleton's Daily Crossword

```
                ¹E
      ²C        R
       A        N
       T        E
      ³T  U  E  S  D  ⁴A  Y
       L        T     B
       E     ⁵M    ⁶P  O  N  D
             A        M         ⁷F  L  O  U  R
             R        I         U
      ⁸R  O  M  P  I  N  G  S  H  I  R  E
             A        A         I
             D        T         T
             U        I         T
             K        O         U
             E        N        ⁹S  W  I  F  T
```

CONGRATULATIONS!

Excellent work, detective! Are you ready for more? There have been some curious happenings aboard a super yacht in the Mediterranean Sea. I could sure use your powers of deduction in solving my next mystery in *Cluedle: The Case of the Golden Pomegranate*, available Fall 2024.